336 HOURS
IN NIGERIA
THE PHENOMENOLOGY
OF A BROKEN NATION

■ It has become necessary to confront realities of the relics of this rich Nation bastardized by brainless despots into political insecurity, economic vagueness, uncontrolled criminality, and communal wretchedness. Knowing Nigeria is one thing; understanding the socio-political structures require a different aptitude.

Dr. Anthony Obi Ogbo Ph.D.

ANTHONY OBI OGBO

336 HOURS
IN NIGERIA
THE
PHENOMENOLOGY
OF A
BROKEN NATION

FIRST EDITION

AMERICAN JOURNAL *of*
TRANSFORMATIONAL LEADERSHIP

Texas International
Guardian Newspapers

AMERICAN JOURNAL *of*
TRANSFORMATIONAL LEADERSHIP

Texas International
Guardian Newspapers

Published in the United States
by the American Journal of Transformational Leadership

© 2012 by Texas International Guardian Newspapers Inc.

Reprinted 2015

First printed in 2012 as Out of Texas: 336 Hours in Motherland

Cover Design | Anthony Obi Ogbo, *Guardian News Network*
Research Intern | Stephanie Adaeze Ogbo
Photographs | *Guardian News Network*

ISBN-13: 978-1517487690

Printed in the United States of America

"A left-over of colonialism which worked relentlessly at destroying the structures of Negro-African civilizations and demarcating boundaries with her own interests as the sole criterion; Federal Nigeria has never since her independence shown the distinctive mark of a united nation. It has been impossible for her to silence tribal rivalries - to achieve the mixture of ethnic and cultures likely to secure national unity."

- Dr. Francois Duvalier,
President of The Republic of Haiti (1957 -1971).

APPRECIATION

It 'takes a village,' and special thanks must go to both the seen and unseen individuals that have contributed in various ways to make this publication possible; Dr. Emeaba Emeaba, Don Okolo, Dr. Charles Nwankwo, Joe Nwokedi, Dr. Rita Kingsley, Dr. Anthony Kingsley, Paul Nwokedi, Nitta Ogu, Stephanie Adaeze Ogbo, Anthony Obieze Ogbo, Editorial staff of *International Guardian*, and *The Guardian News Network.*

For developing my philosophical competencies in management in organizational leadership, special appreciation to the Doctoral Community at the University of Phoenix, especially; Dr. Meredith Ward *(Management Philosophies)*; Dr. Andrew Edelman, *(Critical Thinking)*; Dr. Jane Armstrong, *(Leadership)*; Dr. Michael Mc Intyre *(philosophy)*; Dr. Gregory Berry *(Organizational Theory)*; Dr. Linda De Charon *(Communication Strategies)*, and Dr. Ruby Rouse, Dr. Sushil Jindal, and Dr. Xianbin Li *(Research Strategies)*.

-Anthony Obi Ogbo

CONTENTS

Forward

■ The book's chapters dwell on Nigeria's vision of a united country where we ought to stand in brotherhood even though tribes and tongue may differ, but which has now derailed and is hurtling towards perdition. In each section, scathing criticisms of the players involved in the ruination of the country are laid bare for all to see.

EMEABA EMEABA, PhD.

The epithet Chutzpah, which is Yiddish for brazen arrogance, comes to life in the writings of Anthony Obi Ogbo. It aptly sums up the overwhelming response of folks and miffed readers of his Houston-based *International Guardian* newspaper which has irked and rubbed them every which way in its knack for unearthing and disseminating the truth in its gore and glory. Some of us do not want to hear the truth, and definitely not in the style which only Ogbo pushes it. In writing *336 Hours in Nigeria,* Ogbo is in his elements and should know everything there is to know about Nigeria and Nigerian-style governance including how the country went so wildly astray, since he served as a newspaper person during Nigeria's military interregnum. That's when Ogbo was a hotshot political cartoonist in a Nigeria where writing, or drawing anything that is deemed to embarrass people in office earned you jail time in a brutish gulag.

For those unfamiliar with this author, his choice of topics is analogous to putting a sticky-note that reads "Kick Me" on the back of your shirt; he neither writes for the circus, nor pretends to entertain. *336 Hours in Nigeria* is deep—a psychological composition of the suffering of a Nation which had been fabricated for contingency, rather than built to last. Ogbo's *Three Hundred and Thirty-Six Hours* trip to Nigeria engendered this scrutiny of psychological constituents of this great Nation, her history, politics, leadership, organizational development and structure, and how these concepts correlate her prevailing government complexities.

Talk about patriotism and you are bound to elicit stirs of shock. As a virtue, patriotism is now old-fashioned and going the way of the dodo. Every now and then, we may, on those rarest of occasions, view patriotic sentiments much like the writings of Shakespeare: quaint, heart-warming, and no longer in vogue. In truth, the way we criticize our government can become lopsided and we have come to accept that. But to Ogbo, our country remains worthy of a little down-to-earth criticism with a dash of love, and praise.

336 Hours in Nigeria collects Ogbo's writings—comprising his good, his bad, and his ugly articles and prose narratives—

about his native homeland Nigeria. The chapters stitched together in the classic Ogbo one-thread-at-a-time fashion call readers to have a rethink of the basis for the country Nigeria, and to remember what makes her infamous: a thieving, incompetent leadership that does not know the difference between public money and private money; a corrupt society numbed insensate from government-induced austere circumstances; and an uneducated religious zealotry that threatens to balkanize the country.

The book's chapters dwell on Nigeria's vision of a united country where we ought to stand in brotherhood even though tribes and tongue may differ, but which has now derailed and is hurtling towards perdition. In each section, scathing criticisms of the players involved in the ruination of the country are laid bare for all to see.

Ogbo's background in the media, and management in organizational leadership, adds a unique weight to his perspective, and accounts for some of the book's overwhelmingly bleak, almost phobic depiction of Nigeria as a lost cause. A writer, poet, artist, athlete, Ogbo is also an advocate for the use of the news media to provide the means for cultural expression, community discussion, and debate—supplying news and information and facilitating political engagement.

Ogbo's vast world experience makes the articles and arguments in this book all the more fascinating. His effusive expose—often unsubtle, which reveals the unpopular truths about the dire state of Nigeria—points to what ails Nigeria. Structured into four parts, *336 Hours in Nigeria* demands a physico-psychological effort of a stimulating kind to be read. This book demonstrates the patriotism of shining the light at our flaws in order to inspire us to look for a panacea.

To see Nigeria's gifts afresh makes it clear that Nigerians often take these blessings for granted. This book would be a great addition to the library of anyone who loves organizational development and leadership, history or politics. And it's the perfect balance for the many books published today that focus on what Nigeria is doing wrong.

1

Before I Even Begin

■ I want to exercise this flexibility of using words like *tyranny, dictatorship, despotism, repression*, etc to describe ignorant soldiers who ascended to power through a senseless coup – not 'head of state,' or 'military leader.' The only military leader I understand exists in the army barrack, not in a domain of democratic authority.

A s an old fogey Catholic, I have always confessed my sins only to the priest, but on this page, I must break that tradition to confess my latest predicament. Recently, I have been sandwiched between two worlds: the confraternity of media creative writers, and a contrasting immaculate world of scholarly writers. In this book, I will be myself and approach my narratives from the media paradigm—a theoretical approach of what I know, what I see, how I feel, and how I communicate. A writing approach that respects no rules, but emphasizes an eyewitness account of relevant events; a phenomenological scrutiny of the socio-political truth; philosophical evaluation of critical interpretation of those events that shape our existence as citizens. I love this world. The print-media world; my world of irregular hours, inspired by a cup of black coffee poisoned with two shorts of espresso—a major stimulant that brings out the critical thinking spirit in me. This is the secret behind my inspiration.

Not so for my doctoral demeanor; an appearance that demands piousness, decency, and shear immaculacy - even when I write. This is a point where I have to be cognizant of every word I write – unfortunately every sentence is sanitized of those creative metaphors that normally engage the reader. In this scholarly community, the art of dribbling with words, sentences, or even random anthropomorphisms[1] are not negotiable. Could you believe I would have to verify every word, and attribute it to a credible source? Funny enough, I have to credit it to something or someone even when I sneeze and I have to describe it. I hate writing like the Pope. I am not in Vatican. This is Texas – therefore, I must require more than such bookish values to give a qualitative narration of a politically chaotic environment barbarized by disparaging administrative malady, economic blackout, and social corruption.

I want to call a public officer who steals public fund *a thief,* not *an embezzler*. If freedom should ascribe to civil liberty, why not my zeal to say it as it is? I want to exercise this flexibility of using words like *tyranny, dictatorship, despotism, repression,* etc to describe ignorant soldiers who ascended to power through a senseless coup – not *'heads of state,'* or *'military*

---

(1) **Anthropomorphism:** where human characteristics are attributed to inanimate objects.

leader.' The only military leader I understand exists in the army barrack, not in a domain of democratic authority.

But the good news is that no matter how I write, or how I approach my subjects, the end result centers on true belief. Most philosophers, including those in their graves would agree that an important condition of knowledge is rational or justified belief. Feldman[1] explained that traditional analysis of knowledge (TAK) is that which is formulated through belief, truth, and justification. Horrigan [2] contended that since knowledge is a rapport between thought and reality, and that the end of this rapport is the truth; one can describe philosophy of knowledge as a metaphysical inquiry into truth - therefore, I will explore this truth through self, everyday tactic, and scientific knowledge; and in a similar context, ask for the liberty of leaving behind my scholarly qualities in some areas pertaining to the language of this book.

---

(1) **Feldman, R.** (2003). *Epistemology.* Upper Saddle River, NJ: Prentice Hall.
(2) **Horrigan, Paul. G.** (2005). Philosophy of Knowledge. Retrieved from www.horrigan.angelcities.com/knowledge2.htm

I

PSYCHOLOGY OF INFLUENCE

2

Anatomy of Love, Patriotism, and "Say~it~as~it~is" Attitude

■ If patriotism has anything to do with suffering other people's ignorance, vouching for hard-hearted leaders who would only think for themselves, flying a radiant Nigerian flag over a crowd of empty stomachs, please count me out for I'll remain an obedient and justified prodigal son.

When former United States president John F. Kennedy said in his inaugural address, *"My fellow Americans, ask not what your country can do for you, ask what you can do for your country,"* (January, 1961), he was only expressing the idealistic relevance of patriotism and inexorable support for public service. He wasn't giving a lecture on how to love leaders who could care less about their citizens.

But many national leaders in Africa would attempt use of

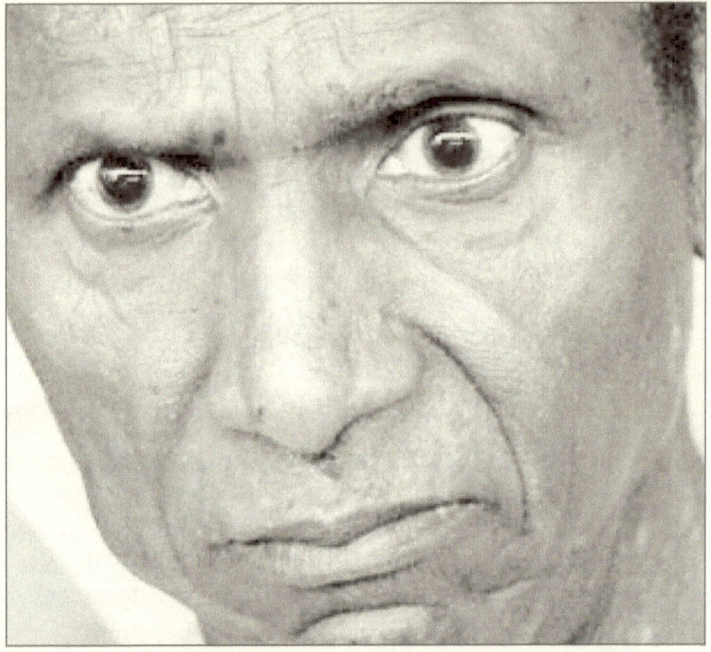

■ Unhealthy Concerns: **President Yar'Adua,** it may be recalled, was a Nigerian leader who had a kidney cancer, yet refused to step down. Rather he unofficially handed over leadership to his ignorant wife, meanwhile making political decisions from an obscure hospital bed in Saudi Arabia.

this quote to manipulate their citizens into love and service to their nation without even providing them with access to the three basic amenities: water, roads, and electricity. Author and philosopher, Mark Twain, contends that *"Patriotism is supporting your country all the time, and your government when it deserves it."* Unfortunately, most Nigerians are yet to witness the manifestation of love when it involves their leaders and their stewardship to the masses.

This was why I was accused of being unpatriotic when I first gave account of my visit to Nigeria in 2006. The very Nigerian citizens for whom I spent time and energy to defend against tyrannical leadership that rendered stagnant the country's progress were the first to call for my head. Then-president of a Houston-based Nigerian organization proclaimed that my publication of the photo of an ailing Nigerian President Umaru Yar'Adua was offensive. His objection read in part:

> "It is a shame that we continue to be part of the people who are putting our country down. We are not utilizing our exposure to western world to better our country. Mr. Tony, as a friend and community leader, I request you take this picture down. It is not representing only Mr. President Yar'Adua, it is representing all of us. I think people like you should be using your time and resources to promote Nigeria."

President Yar'Adua, it may be recalled, was a Nigerian leader who had a kidney cancer, yet refused to step down. Rather, he unofficially handed over leadership to his ignorant wife, while he made political decisions from an obscure hospital bed in Saudi Arabia.

I actually published a photo of him in his enfeebled condition to convince the country that they were being lied to, being told that their president was hale and hearty. A handful thought it unpatriotic, while others commended the idea. Furthermore, my account of an ugly side of the Nigeria's political culture came at a time when others were going to Nigeria and returning with photos of a resplendent Abuja, the capital city, perhaps to give a false impression of their Motherland as a land of milk and honey which, in truth, remains ravaged by hunger, desolation, and self-inflicted wretchedness.

Whereas I sincerely believed that President Yar'Adua's photo was not offensive, I stated categorically that there was nothing as offensive and shameful as the bastardization of democracy and rape of constitution, in one of the continent's most popular countries.

But the major point remained that I was not only born, raised, and educated in Nigeria, but that I could also still close my eyes and describe major intersections in any of its major cities. So I needed no lectures on nationality, especially about such a country where leaders, propagated a murky culture of roguery and socio-political doom.

I was reminded that this was a country where one of the juntas, a president, Sanni Abacha, died surrounded by prostitutes after an overdose of Viagra; that this was a presumably oil-rich state that could not provide basic necessities to its citizens. So what could have been more embarrassing for a country that could not ensure payment of workers' salary than to have a First Lady die on an operating room after undergoing a non-essential plastic surgery? (see page 181).

I am no scholar of patriotism, but I know what patriotism is not. Patriotism is not shielding our problems and suffering the wrath of ignorance in obscurity. Patriotism is not a culture of celebration over taxation without amenities. Patriotism is not pretending to be what you are not. I could go on and on.

Malcolm X (1960) agreed, asserting that *"You're not supposed to be so blind with patriotism that you can't face reality. Wrong is wrong, no matter who says it."* General George S. Patton (1885-1945), in fact, argued that *"If you can't get them to salute when they should salute and wear the clothes you tell them to wear, how are you going to get them to die for their country?"*

Therefore, it becomes a question of reconciling honesty and integrity in a journalistic process. As a realist, I could not bring myself to lie just to prove an unquestioning love for the country I was raised in a love that is not even reciprocated! I believe Mark Twain. I will always support my country, Nigeria, all the time, but will only support the leadership when they wake up from their slumber. Support for my country should not necessitate lying on behalf of corrupt leaders.

Knowledge is about truth. In fact, Feldman's [1] Traditional Analysis of Knowledge (TAK) explains the technicalities of belief, truth, and justification. Hence, my influence is traced back to the era of Greek philosopher, Plato, (427-327 B.C) who probed the difference between knowledge and mere belief thus rejuvenating my attitude towards critical thinking on topical issues.

Consequently, Habermas's [2] theory of "systematically distorted communication" [3] illustrates the practicality of communicative competence. He argues that communication can derail either through manipulation and systematically distortion. "Manipulation is about deception; systematically distorted communication, about self-deception." So why would one lie to be patriotic? My philosophy about love centers on indisputability and reciprocity. The "Tell-it-like-it-is" philosophy is simply an epistemology of truth, ensnared in piousness and nobility.

If patriotism has anything to do with suffering other people's ignorance, vouching for hard-hearted leaders who would only

---

(1) **Feldman, R.** (2003). *Epistemology.* Upper Saddle River, NJ: Prentice Hall.
(2) **Jürgen Habermas** is a Frankfurt School sociologist whose *Theory of Communicative Action* influenced social theory as well as communication research process.
(3) **Johnson, P., & Duberley, J.** (2000). *Understanding management research: An introduction to epistemology.* Thousand Oaks, CA: Sage Publications.

think for themselves, flying a radiant Nigerian flag over a
crowd of empty stomachs, please count me out for I'll remain
an obedient and justified prodigal son.

Love for one's country demands more than flying her flag
in pretense. Indian author and philosopher, Hazrat Inayat
Khan[1] raised my spirits with his description of *Spiritual Liberty* under The Philosophy of Love;

> "When the light of love has been lit, the heart becomes transparent, so that the intelligence of the soul
> can see through it. But until the heart is kindled by
> the flame of love, the intelligence, which is constantly
> yearning to experience life on the surface, is groping
> in the dark."

---

(1) **Khan, H. I.** (1914). *Spiritual Liberty: Love, Human and Divine.* The Philosophy
of Love

3

The Psychology of Native Town, Native Land and Home

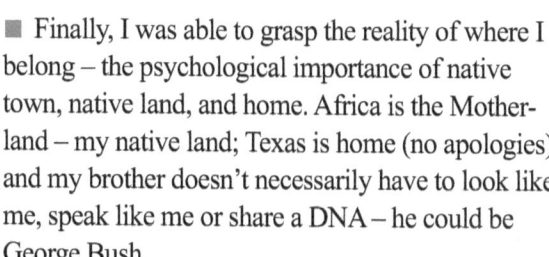

■ Finally, I was able to grasp the reality of where I belong – the psychological importance of native town, native land, and home. Africa is the Mother-land – my native land; Texas is home (no apologies) and my brother doesn't necessarily have to look like me, speak like me or share a DNA – he could be George Bush.

Native town is the town my parents imposed on me. It is traditional in the motherland that one hails from his fa-ther's home domain – their kindred, village, town, Local Government Area, State, and, of course, Country. The Mother's origination didn't really count. I was born in Kaduna, Northern Nigeria, but still, that does not count because my father hails from a town called Nteje, in the East – therefore, I hail from Nteje. This is a non-negotiable custom in Motherland – unlike in some western countries where you hail from your birthplace. I grew up loving this custom and proudly touted my father's home town as my native town. In fact, I never knew about my birth town until my high school era, when I had the opportunity to glance, for the first time, at my birth records. This was when I found out that I was born in a Muslim city in the North, and this was when I sensed that my birthplace bore no relevance to my existence. Hence, I never really knew my father's town because I grew up in another town called Enugu, about 150 miles away. But between life during and after my school years – a 40 year period – I have existed in various cities, in two continents – Africa and North America – grappling with different traditions, environment, and socio-cultural idiosyncrasies.

Today, I am caught up in the realities of dual citizenship – a life in-between two countries, Nigeria and the United States. I grew up in Nigeria and spent half of my life there, whereas the other half of my life is being spent in the United States. I am currently a Texas resident—a United States citizen –dwelling in a diversely congested city of Houston, where I pay taxes.

With this complicated life in multiple cities and various environments enmeshed in different traditions and cultures, a confusion or psychological unpredictability of my prevalent identity may or may not be justified, but it may be excused. So, how do I reconcile the psychosomatic trueness of my native town, native land, and native home? I originated from Nigeria –a country that cares more about her egocentric sobriquet as Motherland's most populous domain than for her citizens—but I reside in the United States – a country that values and understands citizenship as the Pope would to Catholics. So, where is home? One of the founding fathers of the United States, Benjamin Franklin argued that a house is not a home unless it contains food and fire for the mind as well as the body. Additionally, American poet, Robert Frost explained that Home is the place where, when you have to go there, they have to take you in.

However, my trip to Nigeria in 2006 (first in about 20 years) gave me a needed psychological clarification of where I belong, where I should belong, and where I should have belonged in the first place. At the Murtala Muhammed International Airport— my point of entry into Nigeria, the country where I was raised—the Nigerian Customs officers accosted me; they had learnt through my visa that I lost my mom and came for the burial. I had thought I deserved some sort of sympathy, but this was not the case. They were actually excited that I was bereaved and had come from the United States.

The idea was that folks coming for burials bring along monies and other items for ceremonial events. They had organized my luggage and demanded to be bribed, or I would be investigated. Investigated for what? A senior custom officer told me that the event booklets I brought for my mom's burial was printed in the United States, and could be declared a contraband if I did not comply with bribery. In a situation of lawlessness, a situation where the entire system is riddled with shameless corruption, with no protection for the citizens, I was forced to comply. I had found myself in a catastrophic condition where security officers mastermind criminality—a flea market of roguery, hooliganism, and utter uncertainty—service precision means nothing; professionalism does not count, and possibly, life does not mean a thing in this province.

This was how I went, and the beginning of what I went through. But what about coming back? It was through Hartsfield-Jackson Atlanta International Airport. The immigration officer who screened me was a White man. He glanced at my passport and saw the reason for my trip. He looked at me and asked, "How was your mother's burial?" "Hectic, but it went fine" I replied. He stamped and handed me my passport, and said, "I'm sorry about your mom." The whole exercise took less than 10 minutes. This moment created a sharp contrast compared to the encounter with my presumably immigration 'brothers' in Lagos. The approach, sharpness, and the empathy he exhibited emitted a show of professionalism and service excellence. Yet the compassionate words from presumably a 'White stranger' touched my heart and gave me an entirely different food for thought.

Then again, I came out and asked myself, where is my home, and who are my people? Activist, Malcolm X said, *"I believe in the brotherhood of all men, but I don't believe in wasting brotherhood on anyone who doesn't want to practice it with me. Brotherhood is a two-way street."* Immediately, I found out that my brother was that White immigration officer in Atlanta, whereas the bullies at the Lagos airport were not really my brothers, but hooligans that looked like me. Finally, I was able to grasp the reality of where I belong – the psychological importance of native town, native land, and home. Africa is the Motherland – my native land; Texas is home (no apologies) and my brother doesn't necessarily have to look like me, speak like me or share a DNA – he could be George Bush.

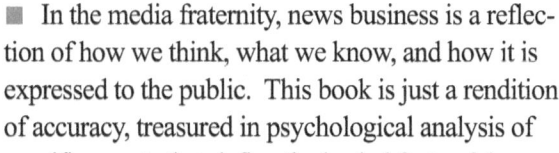

4

Individual Epistemology: Has the Civil War Influenced my Reports and Views about Nigeria?

■ In the media fraternity, news business is a reflection of how we think, what we know, and how it is expressed to the public. This book is just a rendition of accuracy, treasured in psychological analysis of specific events that define the buried facts of the Nigerian Nationhood.

Three individuals, Nigerians from three major regions, East, West, and North, in a discussion forum about Nigeria's past history would argue differently about the civil war. The Easterner would speak as a victim of a war that saw the starving and slaying of millions of her citizens, including children, elders, handicaps, and families. The Northerner would

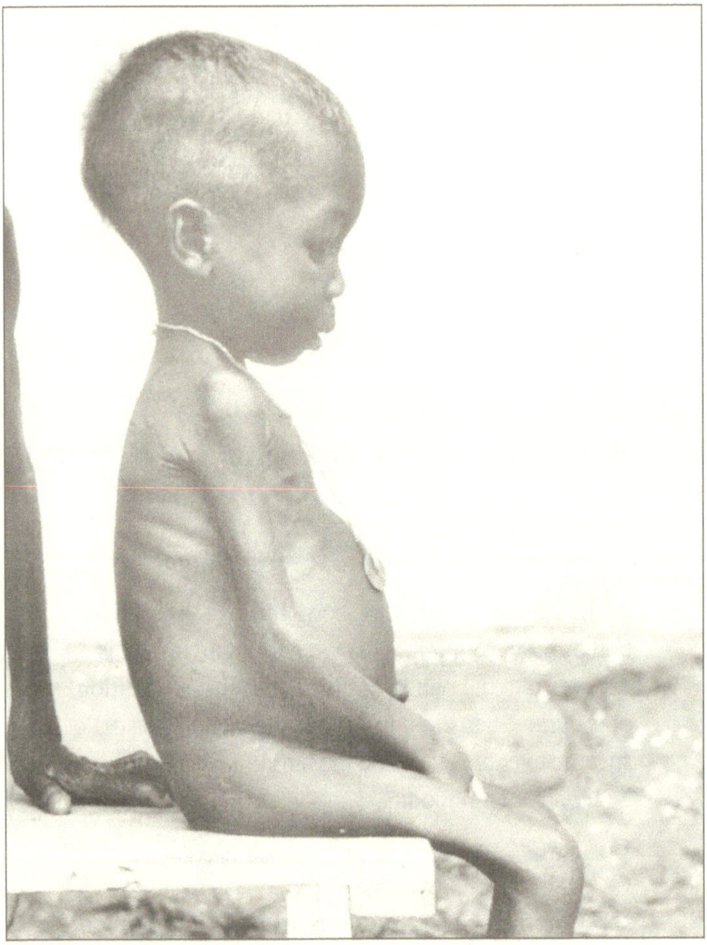

■ **What I Saw:** "It was a sorry sight to see my fellow kids crawling with protruded bellies, and emaciated body frames visibly revealing their ribs."

The **Civil War:** Photo of a child suffering the effects of severe hunger and malnutrition during the Nigerian offensive. *Photo: Academic Dictionaries and Encyclopedias.*

speak from the perspective of the patriot who loved this country so much as long as she controlled the political powers, whereas the Westerner, presumably economic beneficiary of this war, would dismiss any ugly past "because we have to move forward." This underscores the negative impact of inability of this country to coordinate the unity of her tribally diverse post-civil war generation.

Psychologically speaking, it is obvious that different experiences underscore different analysis. For instance, those Nigerians who lived during this war and never experienced it would speak from *Google* and *Wikipedia*. Those who remained overseas while the Igbo people in Eastern Nigeria underwent genocide would speak from *TimeLife Documentaries;* and those who saw, or fought the war in Biafra would speak with emotions, or anger. Nonetheless, the most compelling opinion emanates from an eyewitness account of the individuals who fought in the region called Biafra; those victims who survived the refugee camps, who thrived in forest region of various villages for thirty months under thunderous sounds of shelling booms, and rattling of the AK-47 assault raffles.

The government had since the end of this horrific war outlawed honest discussions about horrible deeds of the event; distorted historical facts that justified claims of genocide, and even honored those who directed these atrocities. To render her actions most hypocritical, Nigeria believes that it is okay to teach students the history and wars in the Roman Empire; the World Wars; Osei Tutu Wars of the 17th century; 19th century wars of Asante and the British; the history of slavery, etc, but would consider it a taboo to offer history lessons of her own major war. This is why it may be difficult for every Nigerian to love Nigeria as a country.

In knowledge theories, it is universal that personal beliefs about what we know influence our attitude and behavior. Age, intellect, or intricacy of issues notwithstanding, personal reflection of knowledge shapes our conclusions. As we watch the television, listen to our leaders, participate in various life-related discussions, or engage in other knowledge claims, we face major challenges about the credibility or authenticity of our phenomenological renditions.

We tend to learn what we perceive as the truth, which makes it imperative to believe that learning is impacted by knowledge and beliefs. This personal conviction and conjectures are ingredients that may shape my individual epistemology. Therefore, as a journalist who invests much time in reporting stories from events, editing stories from various correspondents, analyzing stories, and events, and documenting facts about occurrences; the technicalities of truth, knowledge, and beliefs; how I know, what I know, and the manner in which I know, compliment my thinking and cognitive capacities.

I am a child victim of the Nigerian civil war; a shocking event ignored by the international community, and scorned by the Nigerian government. No wonder, ever since the death of Ikemba Odumegwu Ojukwu,[1] in November, 2011, the print, electronic, and the social media have been agog with analysis and historical compositions about this leader, and his unfulfilled dreams of the Biafran nationhood. With commentaries controlled by emotions, and different socio-political interests, it becomes difficult at times to comprehend the physical and

---

(1) **Chukwuemeka Odumegwu Ojukwu** was the leader of the defunct Republic of Biafra from 1967 to 1970 and a Nigerian politician from 1983 to 2011. He died, 26 November 2011 (aged 78) in the United Kingdom.

psychological realities of this three year bloody combat that decimated the people of the Eastern Nigeria, their culture, and their prospects as a region.

An epistemological analysis of knowledge and how it relates to my quest for critical thinking demands specifically, scholarly identification of my possible sources. Of course, knowledge could be derived through perception, memory, testimony, introspection, reasoning, and rational insight.[1] It may not be enough to report or analyze events based on perception or reasoning or unverified testimonies, as I must also evaluate other dependable sources, and reconcile them with what I saw with my eyes. It is a fact that documented information could be misrepresented, or misinterpreted, but the legitimacy of an eyewitness which I express in some parts of this book remains the truth, the whole truth, and an unquestionably, a clean-cut reality.

For instance, as a child victim of the Biafran civil war, my testimony comes from memory rather than *Google*. As a 6-year old before the war, and a 9-year old after, who also survived the post war era, it is sometimes difficult to sit on the same panel of discussion with peers who lived normal lives in the same period, in the war-free Nigerian territory. They would make you feel guilty, or look at you as some unpatriotic nincompoop - a Biafran sorry loyalist. Sometimes they would argue from the rear in shear fallacy, or even recite doctored Internet information or adulterated opinions retrieved from nowhere. Yet, I would remain unshaken as I unleash horrible feelings impelled by memories of guns, blood, and human skulls in its irrefutable exactitude.

Without reaching for any search tools, I could speak from

---

(1) **Feldman, R.** (2003). *Epistemology.* Upper Saddle River, NJ: Prentice Hall.

memory of this horrible past that I saw it all with my 'naked' eyes; that I was in Kindergarten when the initial war campaign started, and Coal City was under bombardment by fighter and bomber jets operated by the White mercenaries. Trenches were dug in the schools to provide save areas against fighter plane attacks. The teachers would always remove our white shirts, and throw us into these trenches anytime the bomb alerts went off. This was the initial stage. Therefore, I could speak about this war with an authentic knowledge of a victim. This is why, in this contest, epistemology remains the study of knowledge, with core relevance of understanding the process of knowing, thus drawing a thin line between cases where we know and cases where knowledge lacks.

Without doubt, the sight of civil war, and struggle as a child in the post war era created in me an entirely different mindset when talking about this country. For instance, as a child during this war, I witnessed dead bodies, wounded soldiers, hungry and sick refugees eager to eat just about anything. In Achalla, Awka province, where I survived the war, refugees trooped in thousands, and relief workers fed them with corn meal. A bowl a day could do for a person, and when supplies ran out, refugees walked round the town for anything chewable. I saw refugees feed on lizards, insects, rats, and just about anything that could ease a devastating need for survival. I also saw sick ones who got so sick out of malnutrition or other strange diseases. This was the time I knew about Kwashiorkor - a severe energy malnutrition typified by insufficient protein consumption. It was a sorry sight to see my fellow kids crawling with protruded bellies, and emaciated body frames visibly revealing their ribs. Sights like this are enough to make a man speak with a clinched fist, or hands balled for a dwell, even where there is no opponent.

As a child I stood awake with others, sleepless at nights for fear of unexpected bombardment. I knew what assault rifles looked like; saw how bombers descended from nowhere and dropped bombs at market places. Yes, I could recall the day we were playing kite in grand dad's gigantic compound and two bomber planes descended from nowhere and flew over. The noise alone could till a rocky ground – then as these flying equipment vanished into a cloudy sky, a shocking sound trailed it. Moments, later we learnt that a busy Otuocha Market was bombed, and bodies were crushed like roaches – eloquent of the fact that the Nigerian troops targeted civilians. This was just a tip out of a devastating 30-month horrific experience as a child who did not go to the war field, but suffered it all.

Yet the worst was yet to come after the war in 1970. We were hauled back to a city we left three years back. A city now devastated by the war was left without basic amenities. School buildings, churches, and homes were torn apart by shelling and other destructive devises of the war. I attended school under the trees at times and classes shifted at intervals to secure a comfortable shadowed spot. Pupils brought their desks to school because there was just none at the schools at the time. Kids went to school barefooted, while others stayed home because their parents could not afford tuition, books, and uniforms.

Now, this was the war I saw, and survived. Yet it is more distressing to have gone through this ordeal as a child without a single post-war traumatic therapy. I could just close my eyes and think of what it would be like for a young child to be in similar traumatic situations. He could feel totally helpless and passive. He could have the most difficulty with their intense physical and emotional reactions; he could just lose out in the process of coping with ongoing threats to his survival; he could not afford to trust, relax or fully explore his own feelings, ideas or interests.

Young trauma victims often come to believe there is something inherently wrong with them; that they are at fault, unlovable, hateful, helpless and unworthy of protection and love. Such feelings lead to poor self-image, self-abandonment, and self-destructiveness. Ultimately, these feelings could leave them vulnerable to subsequent trauma. Yet, here I am still standing, pledging allegiance to Nigeria with all sense of patriotism—a nation still being governed by some of the leaders that masterminded the devastating genocide I survived almost 41 years ago.

Therefore, I say that as a child, scaling through this period as a hopeless survivor is bound to shape my tongue differently discussing this Nation. Knowledge is a mystery, and information acquired in such excruciating circumstances remain indelible in my pitiful seat of sensation. The origin or mechanics of human knowledge is not a misleading notion. Locke[1] was right in his thoughts that the mind is blank at birth but become fully engaged with information from experience. I must have been born with a clear mind that later become engaged by the thing within the environment. In contrast, it may have been a clear case of innate ideas. My mind may have been equipped with essential concepts that necessitate knowledge, separately from the senses.

But the truth is that my war experience is one of those ugly pasts that shape my current attitude regarding the philosophical

---

(1) **Locke, J.** (1690). An Essay Concerning Human Understanding. Retrieved from www.ilt.columbia.edu

questions about brotherhood and progress in Nigeria. Besides the constitution—a set of ambiguous written rules of governance—what actually makes us a Nation? Besides geographical locations and neighborhood boundaries, how spiritual are all tribes related? What are those values that bind our comradeship?

Purpose and major source of philosophic questioning is the wisdom of doubt – the tendency to wonder just about anything. Philosophy juggles the mind with puzzlement, surprise, astonishment about the mystery and reality of oneself, humanity, and reality of general existence. Philosophies materialize out of an eagerness to follow the call of human cerebral oddity, allowing a formulation of questions that guide curiosity toward comprehension of specific problems.

Socrates, for instance, emphasized as philosophical purpose, the gain of self-knowledge, through theoretical lucidity. Plato sees the concept as the discovery of certainty or utter truth, through conflicting notions. Aristotle contends that philosophy began with the perception of fear and conjecture. Descartes sees philosophy as the illumination of ultimate truth through skepticism, whereas Locke sees philosophy as psychoanalysis of thoughts stocked in the brain.

A claim of psychosomatic effects of the civil war in my judgments of issues about Nigeria reflect evidentialism – a theory of knowledge which justifies that factual knowledge is entirely a matter of evidence. Contemporary philosophers have rightly indoctrinated the traditional values of truth and accuracy into the chronicles of the modern era - inspiring the hypothesis that conforms that a belief must be accurate to work, and becomes fallacious where it fails to work. My Individual knowledge of Nigeria, and her surmounting disputes are evidential revelations of a quest for clarity, accuracy, and relevance; a systematic embrace of story depth, and intellectual fairness.

These are the epistemological values that would propel my thoughts; a philosophy that correlates Feldman's[1] Traditional Analysis of Knowledge that would reveal the technicalities of belief, truth, and justification; a concept that determines the extent of human knowledge with truth-seeking questions about what I know. In the media fraternity, news business is a reflection of how we think, what we know, and how it is expressed to the public. This book is just a rendition of accuracy, treasured in psychological analysis of specific events that define the buried facts of the Nigerian Nationhood.

(1) **Feldman, R.** (2003). *Epistemology*. Upper Saddle River, NJ: Prentice Hall.

336 HOURS
IN NIGERIA
THE PHENOMENOLOGY OF A BROKEN NATION

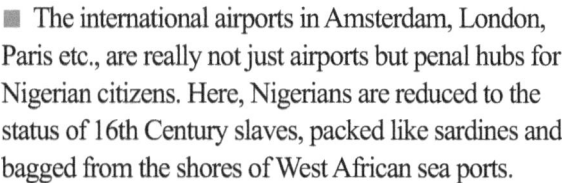

5

Confronting the Relics of a Rich Nation

■ The international airports in Amsterdam, London, Paris etc., are really not just airports but penal hubs for Nigerian citizens. Here, Nigerians are reduced to the status of 16th Century slaves, packed like sardines and bagged from the shores of West African sea ports.

To an average Nigerian living in the United States as of 2006, Delta Airline was all that. The reason being that at the period, this airline remained the only toy that flew directly from the United States to Nigeria. It is a blessing not to fly through any of the European routes. The international airports in Amsterdam, London, Paris etc., are really not just airports but penal hubs for Nigerian citizens. Here, Nigerians are reduced to the status of 16th Century, packed like sardines and bagged from the shores of West African sea ports. Airport officials at these European cities are trained specifically to deal with Nigerians, their travel documents; their luggages, tribes, accents and most importantly, their attitudes. They understand Nigerian food items more than the village grocery hawkers; and can tell exactly where those food items are hidden.

Goodbye to Texas

Amongst a list of these connection hubs, Nigerians understand that the Heathrow Airport is the worst domain in passenger profiling. If color doesn't give you up, your attire would. Even as a Nigerian, you decide to dress like the Duke of Edinburgh, your accent would surely give you away. Yes, Heathrow Airport has such a reputation – a reputation for racial intolerance, linguistic discrimination, and narrow-minded attitude toward Nigerians.

This is really a big airport, covering a land mass of about 1,227 hectares; two runways, and an average air transport movements 1,305[1]. It may be recalled that it was the British that perpetrated an age of slave trade that shifted into the age of colonization. It is a historical fact that by the mid-18th century, Britain had the monopoly of slavery, and reserved the sole license to ship black slaves from Africa to Spanish controlled territories in America, in the Treaty of Utrecht of 1713. From this slave era till this age, British dominance of issues of Africa; their philosophy to "explore, conquer, and rule African peoples" remain unshaken.

Treatment of people of color at the Heathrow Airport brings

---

(1) Information from **heathrowairport.com;** official website of the Heathrow Airport.

back that torturing slave memory; an epitome of oppression through unfair dichotomy and psychological persecution of Black folks with African accent. It gets worse by the hour; thus English officials at the Heathrow Airport can tell Nigerians by merely looking at them. Sometimes, they can stare at you and call you by your tribe – "Ibo? Ok step forward, and place your bag right here; OK Madame, I can see you have three names – Ngozi, Ngo, Ngozichukwu; now, are you aware you are in violation?" The voice alone is a secretion of a high-pitched, croaky sound with intimidating vibes – enough to make an innocent passenger pass out in guilt. My God!!

This is how bad these officers are trained—a cluster of selected bullies brainwashed with prejudicial indoctrination – that all Nigerians are dishonest. Thus, the Nigerian citizen is often scorned, humiliated, and psychologically tortured – so bad that she could plead guilty by just hearing her name. In fact, as a Nigerian, moving around these European airports in a traditional attire means exposing your hated nationality; it means inviting an interrogation that might translate into unprecedented delays; those delays that could ground a passenger for another day. Awfully enough, those horribly looking police guard dogs are equally trained to detect Nigerians, their goods and chattels. An average police dog, for instance, can detect a bag of *Egusi*[1] before a package of hard drugs. This explains why it may be easier for drug peddlers to smuggle their contrabands than a half tuber of Abakiliki yam or a bag of yellow *Garri*[2] from Benin.

---

(1) **Egusi seeds** (melon): a wild member of the gourd family of plants is popular in Western Africa.
(2) **Garri:** West African food (tapioca made from cassava tubers.) Popular in Nigeria, Cameroon, Sierra Leone, and Ghana.

Repack
area

■ **The Heathrow Monarchy:** As chaotic as it could be, trained officers are a cluster of selected bullies brainwashed with prejudicial indoctrination – that all Nigerians are dishonest. **Inset:** twitted photo of an isolated zone marked as 'Repack Area' is for Nigerian passengers only.

This is exactly why Nigerians loved it when Delta opted for a direct flight to Nigeria. They were prepared to pay through their brains to make sure that they avoided any two-tier route trip through Europe. Nigerians had embraced Delta as a remedy, and trusted this airline with their money; adopting it as their non-stop home-going carrier.

The joy was obvious: anything but Heathrow. However; all

that glitters is not gold. Delta is no saint compared to the British Airways, and their Heathrow 'slave torture yard.' Delta knew Nigerians in America had the money, but were longing for more convenient service, so they jumped into the market with the sole aim to generate a cash flow.

Delta apparently had a different structure with their Nigerian operations. Nigerians all over cities in the United States are collected like grains and dumped at the Hartsfield-Jackson Atlanta International Airport, the home of Delta, for an 11-hour flight to Nigeria. Similarly, those passengers are brought back and dumped at the same airport without concrete arrangement for a connection flight back to their original cities. You can see them walking around at the terminals exhausted; seniors are left to nap on the floors, or uncomfortable airport waiting seats, shivering in cold, and using their hand luggage as pillows. What if you are not a Nigerian? You are offered a hotel if you missed a connection flight and have to fly the next day; or given a free pillow if you have to wait for hours. My God, it's not easy to be a Nigerian!

The disparity in the service process was conspicuously troubling. These airlines care the least about their Nigerian passengers - for instance, in 2009, the Nigeria government threatened to sanction British Airways (BA) and Delta Airlines over poor service and the maltreatment of Nigerian passengers. Then Aviation Minister, Babatunde Omotoba, claimed BA and Delta Airlines treated Nigerian passengers in violation of the rules of the International Civil Aviation Organization (ICAO), citing how a London bound flight was delayed for more than six hours as a result of technical problems the aircraft had encountered twice within an hour. Honorable minister, Omotoba consequently accused Delta Airlines of flying its Nigerian route with old aircrafts that could not be used on other routes. In fact, Nigerian

■ **Delta's Nigerian Routes:** The disparity in service process was conspicuously troubling. Nigerian's then Aviation Minister, Honorable Babatunde Omotoba, consequently accused Delta Airlines of flying its Nigerian route with old aircrafts that could not be used for other routes.

Civil Aviation Authority (NCAA) concluded plans to summon Delta Airlines for allegedly using "scrappy" aircraft on the Nigerian route, adding that BA was also guilty of a similar practice.

Nigerians are not easy to deal with either: Checking-in Nigerian passengers require extra recruits, process, and regulations. Their luggage alone would flunk any safety rules, coupled with an egocentric attitude that could only work in African villages. For instance, the most common baggage rules are size-limits; these rules written on various publications, that bags over 50 lbs (23 kg) are considered overweight, whereas bags over 62 inches (157 cm) are oversized. Some Nigerian passengers would of course bring heavy bags weighing almost double the accepted sizes, thereby creating serious delays in the checking-in process.

Have you really been in a Delta flight headed for Lagos during the Christmas season? Ramshackle Delta Airline is loaded to the brim, with passengers talking so loud and snacking in horribly stinking African delicacies. Do you know what it means to dole out a rubber plate of *Ugba* and *Stockfish* in a flight? For goodness sake this stuff stinks like a dead body, and I would pity passengers from other cultures having to endure such environment.

Yet - those are demands of having to manage cultural diversity; the ability to study the cultural components of an organization and fashion out appropriate management strategies to accommodate stakeholders. If an Airline can make adequate arrangement to accommodate pets, they should also be able to accommodate people's way of life, including how they interact and what they eat.

This is where Delta got it wrong in handling their Nigerian operation: letting their appetite for profitability overshadow their passion for unmatched service delivery; undermining the needs of their Nigerian passengers, and in fact leaving them vulnerable to bribery and other forms of extortion at their service centers at the Nigerian Airports; poor connection flights arrangements; and dehumanization of their Nigerian passengers at their Hartsfield-Jackson Atlanta domain.

■ The **Murtala Muhammed International Airport:** I could feel even before the announcement for landing preparations that I was minutes away
from my destination. How did I know we were in Lagos? I looked
through the window and saw the city already in total blackout. You can
feel the power interruption, which is normal in this country. *Photo: Ahmet
KOCAK, Aug 31, 2006.*

Welcome to Africa

I really did not fly Delta: I did not fly first class either, because I knew I had to pay bills when I got back, but on board
KLM - Royal Dutch Airline - I saw myself headed straight to

Nigeria on a planned 14-day trip - three hundred and thirty six hours approximately. It was partly a fact-finding journey in a region I last visited in over almost 18 years at the time. Praise God I made it back.

From Amsterdam to my final destination, Lagos was a six-hour trip in a 747 airbus flying more than 33,000 feet above the Sahara, only interrupted by mild turbulence that would hardly spill your coffee. I counted my time by minutes until we finally approached Lagos in the late hours of the day. I could feel even before the announcement for landing preparations that I was minutes away from my destination. How did I know we were in Lagos? I looked through the window and saw the city already in total blackout. You can feel the power interruption, which is normal in this country.

The airport looked no different from its chaotic standards years ago. In fact, it had gotten worse as uncontrolled security officers and unidentified thugs intimidate passengers for bribes. They will take anything for a bribe...money, food, snacks, candy - especially when it is foreign product. A five dollar tip to a custom officer would guide you through any number of check-points without a search - even if you carry explosives. I already know – I understand this region more than the Pope would know Vatican.

At the airport immigration checkpoints were officers sitting behind some computer system, recording information from visitors. But the effectiveness of this system or accuracy of information provided by passengers becomes another issue. This may not sound good at all for a worldwide war and campaign against terror - but, I offered a destination address that does not exist and was ushered into the country. I may be al-Qaeda. No wonder Boko Haram terrorists are playing poker with Nigeria's

■ **This is Lagos:** The chaotic traffic would give anyone a severe headache. God – So much noise and you would think Ted Nugent is having a live concert. Motorbikes transport passengers infest all corners of the roads, barely abiding by the least of road-safety measures. A crash helmet means nothing, as these motorcycles compete with cars and trucks on narrow ugly roads and bridges.
Photo: Anthony Ogbo/International Guardian.

internal security and loving it.

I was in fact welcome to Lagos City, the most populous in Nigeria, the largest country in Africa with a 5-Dollar bribe. This city is commercial to the core with metropolitan area estimated at 300 square kilometers, encompassing a number of islands endowed with creeks and a lagoon. Judging by high volume commerce and inhabitation, Lagos is projected to be one of the world's five largest cities. And this happened to be my entry point.

I knew where I was. I could smell it. I knew I had stepped into a pit of uncertainty, ranging from constant power interruptions to unmanaged roads, riddled with large potholes and hungry-looking traffic cops boldly extorting small change from poor transporters. Road-side hawkers overrun the streets, and besiege cars like hungry vultures. It was like the Gaza Strip on a typical riot day; a jinxed environment suffused with ugly and polluted air; humidity level or even visibility would upset any aspirated psychrometer.

The chaotic traffic would give anyone a severe headache. God – So much noise and you would think Ted Nugent is having a live concert. Motorbikes transport passengers at all corners of the roads, barely abiding by the least of road-safety measures. A crash helmet means nothing, as these motorcycles compete with cars and trucks on narrow ugly roads and bridges. Ironically, I never saw a single accident. God is good!

Road warning signs were non-existent, as major views were littered with badly placed billboards and graffiti. There were no regular street signs - yet somehow people find their ways. Street hawkers outnumber motorists and more or less infest every intersection like killer bees. Everything is sold here, and I'm sure human heads might be available by special request. In fact, one can cross off an entire household shopping list without a trip to the mall. Everything is sold on these major roads; every business too, including foreign exchange transactions - just ask.

Most Nigerian cities were better off during the colonial days - yet these Nigerian leaders would always invoke the colonial history as being disadvantageous to their progress. The Colonial masters handled Nigeria from 1807, when Great Britain abolished the slave trade. Britain's increasing involvement in this region prevailed through treaties and arrangements with re-

■ **Negotiating Bribery:** hungry-looking traffic cops boldly extorting money from poor transporters. *Photo: gistmania.com*

gional rulers; and as of late 1865, Great Britain took a more active role with the Nigerian protectorates. Antagonists of this agenda, however, saw the colonial agenda as manipulative. For instance, the colonialists were everything from exploiters of African natural resources to instigating division among tribes.

Critically thinking from another perspective, on the so called colonialism, Colonial Master, Frederick John Lugard was made the Governor of Hong Kong (1907–1912) and Governor-General of Nigeria (1914–1919) - but Look at Hong Kong and look at Nigeria. Whitman's rule before independence was more transparent in terms of developments. At least there were amenities to complement taxes. There were lights, water, and roads system. All that was needed were improvement of those developments through expansion and maintenance of the colonial legacy.

Today, more than 51 years after colonialism, things have taken a turn for the worst. Even with more revenue coming from petroleum, the central government could not boast of one out of the three basic amenities, while the leaders flourish in riches out of embezzled public funds. Energy and water access, sewage, transportation, and housing have all been adversely affected by a failed stewardship.

International Monetary Fund (IMF) in 2005 published what was tagged "Poverty Reduction Strategy Paper about Nigeria, and in a more qualitative analysis echoed a similar concern;

> "Nigeria's legacy of mismanagement and corrupt governance has encouraged many people to seek ways of sharing the national cake instead of helping bake it. By 1999 corruption was practically institutionalized. Government was widely regarded as a provider of large contracts, distributed by officers in power to people wealthy enough to buy their influence. This was particularly so in the case of the oil industry. Over time, the judiciary became intimidated, as the rich and powerful manipulated laws and regulations to their advantage. Instead of engaging in productive activities that would help our economy grow, people chose instead to peddle their influence and position. The legitimacy and stability of the state suffered, as people began to devise ways to survive that lay outside the law."

41

■ Fixing a broken-down **Power Generation**
Consistency in power supply lacks in total measures, with power interruptions occurring at least five times a day. An average taxpaying citizen
owns a power generator for electricity. Hundreds of such plants are scattered in congested neighborhoods, generating so much noise and emission that they offend late evening sanity. *Photo: NaijaLife.*

In Lagos for instance, unlike most other cities in Nigeria, about 90% of the population has access to electricity, with the city consuming 45% of the energy of the country. But consistency in power supply lacks in total measures, with power interruptions occurring at least five times a day. Despite the region's endowment of water, the city suffers from an acute and worsening water supply shortage. This, coupled with inadequate sewage systems render some parts of this city offensively unhygienic; and so disappointing that at local public places including airports, hawkers hang around washrooms offering toilet papers for fees.

Individuals have actually lost faith in the government and have resorted to providing their own water and power supply. An average taxpaying homeowner owns a power generator for electricity. Hundreds of such plants are scattered in congested neighborhoods, generating so much noise and emission that they offend late evening sanity. The shortage applies to water supply as residents set up their own boreholes and buy water supply from private water tankers.

What goes around comes around – thus, the leaders that perpetrate evil in this country are not exonerated from the dire repercussions. For instance, in 2008, a member of Kano State House of Assembly, Alhaji Muktar Liman Rogo, member of an All Nigeria Peoples Party (ANPP), died after he sustained severe burns from a running generator at the legislators' quarters in Kano. Nigeria's *ThisDay* reported Rogo, aged 43, caught fire in his residence at the legislators' quarters at Faraway village along Maiduguri road while trying to refill a running engine generator. Poor Rogo: his soul would surely rest in peace, but what explanation would he offer to St. Peter [1] at the heaven's gate as to why he could not legislate constant electricity supply

43

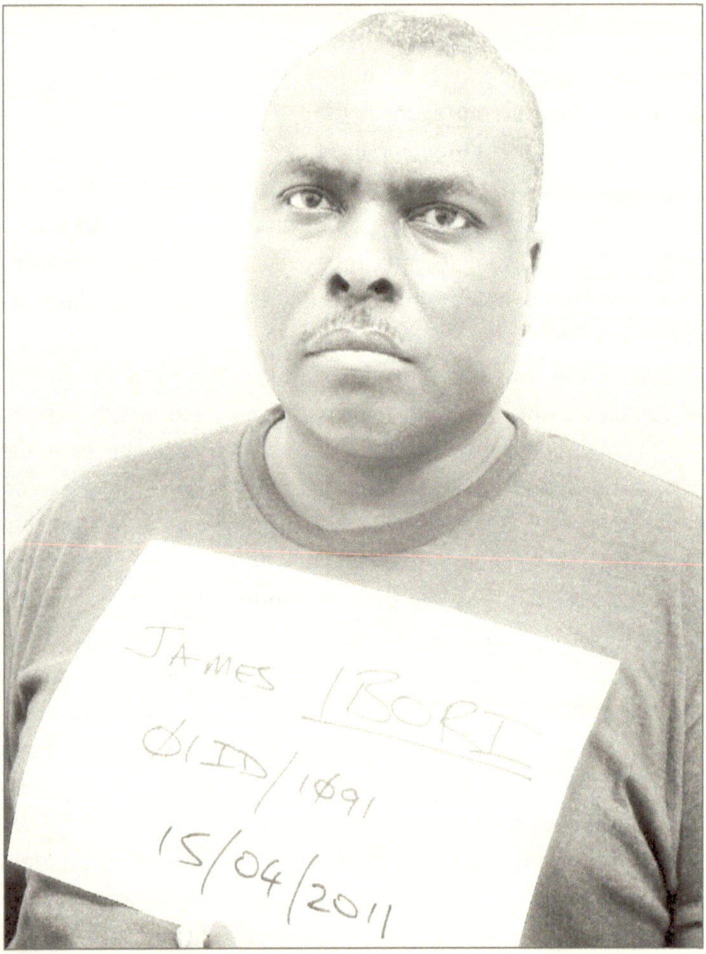

■ **He Was a Governor...** A proven lack of accountability, discipline and corruption in all corridors of leadership remain cancerous to the entire system, crippling progress and stagnating socio-economic development. This is a mug shot of a former governor of Nigeria's oil-rich Delta state, **James Ibori,** who received a 13-year jail sentence after admitting fraud of nearly £50m. *The guardian,* UK reported how Ibori worked his way up from being a cashier in a London DIY store to becoming governor of Nigeria's Delta region. *Photograph: Metropolitan police/PA*

for his constituency?

So where is the government? There are three major governmental set-ups - the federal, state and local, operating in a full-fledged democratic system. But a proven lack of accountability, discipline, and corruption in all corridors of leadership remain cancerous to the entire system, crippling progress and stagnating socio-economic development in a naturally endowed region that has taken in an estimated $300 billion in oil revenue since the 1970s, and is among the top 10 oil producers.

Reality Check

According to the United Nations, Nigeria's producing states receive just 13 percent of the revenue from the sale of oil. This is a country where the vast majority of the 130 million people live in poverty. The relatively small share of oil profits for the producing regions has left a bitter taste and prompted a rise in militant movements. In 2006, a Finance Minister, Nenadi Usman, admitted that Nigeria has lost $Bo in oil revenue in the past year due to increasing violence in its Niger Delta region. Activities of these militant groups demanding more control of Nigeria's oil revenue have visibly reflected cuts in oil exports. IMF continued in its narrative studies:

> "Past governments allowed oil income to influence spending: when income was high, spending was high, while dips in oil prices were treated as temporary. To-

---

(1) **Page 43.** Christians believe **Jesus** gave to Saint Peter, **keys of the Kingdom of Heaven** empowering him to take binding actions. According to the Gospel of Matthew (16:19) Jesus says to Peter, "I will give you the keys of the kingdom of heaven, and whatever you bind on earth shall be bound in heaven, and whatever **you** loose on earth shall be loosed in heaven."

gether with poor coordination between federal and state governments in budgeting and expenditure, this practice led to spiraling debt. Today all tiers of government spend far more than they earn: the deficit for the past five years alone amounts to more than N1 trillion. With external and domestic debt of 70 percent of GAD, current revenue is largely eaten up just by debt service."

This again raised some critical questions about patriotism in the midst of economic misfortune perpetrated by leaders who do not just care. Then the bitter truth came up. If patriotism has anything to do with suffering other people's ignorance or vouching for mean-hearted leaders who would only think for themselves, please count me out. If patriotism is flying a good-looking green-white-green flag on untarred roads leading to nowhere – please count me out for I would rather remain an obedient and justified prodigal son; a Harwin Street die-hard Bayou City road trotter; one of those Texans that hate Governor Rick Perry, but would still pay allegiance to the Wranglers, the Levi slim jeans, and those fierce-looking boots – the Lone Star's State traditional have on. Hence, with every scrap of sincerity and prostration to my forefathers in Africa, I still love my native land, but I remain a true Houstonian and I'm loving it!

Reminded of the shameful taxation without both representation and amenities in the Motherland's most populous country, my mind began to search for resolutions. For a moment, I appreciated The United States Internal Revenue Services. I vowed to pay my taxes on time, privileged to live in a more civilized society where at least the basic amenities of life were obligatory - an entitlement for the taxpayer. I closed my eyes and imagined myself in Texas digging a borehole behind my house to supply myself water, or servicing power generators to give myself light. God...not in my lifetime.

This town called Engud is no exception. Nicknamed the Coal City, a state capital in the eastern part of Nigeria, underdevelopment due to mismanagement becomes obvious. Visibility was almost zero, not because of fogs or any weather mishap, but due to a cloud of dust rising from the red earth of untarred roads posing an immediate health hazed. All cars were virtually brown in color having been suffused by unfriendly dusts. Pot holes on the roads are as big as landslide cracks.

I visited a few schools I knew in the past and got the shock of my life. Structures were worse than before, and dormitories were left with broken roofs and without windows. Missionaries built most of these schools during the colonial days almost 60 to 80 years ago. Today, these schools exist with the same initial structures without undergoing any major renovation or maintenance. The walls are exactly the same archaic brick and cement surface erected by the White man in their days – and now, one can see with me - why I believed that Nigeria needed to bring back the Colonial Masters.

In this Coal City, the government touted a pricey landmark tunnel as its major achievement in improving road standards and safety. A visit to *Eaton Tunnel* revealed another disappointment from a leadership that has failed its taxpayers. It is a minisize overhead bridge erected on the wrong side of the city where there is very little traffic. It looks like an overpass built over a dead end: I pulled over and wept – about how public officers could be so callous, greedy, and heartless.

The shocking revelation about every major local government in this country, especially in the south is that there is so much money in the system, thousands of development contracts exchange hands; there are budgets and large money expenditures,

■ **Ebeano Tunnel:** In this Coal City, the government touted a pricey landmark tunnel as its major achievement in improving road standards and safety. A visit to *Ebeano Tunnel* revealed another disappointment from a leadership that has failed its taxpayers. It's a mini-size overhead bridge erected on the wrong side of the city where there is very little heavy traffic. It looks like an overpass built over a dead end: I pulled over and wept for a second – about how public officers could be so callous, greedy, and heartless.

Photo: Anthony Obi Ogbo/International Guardian.

yet nothing gets done. I ran into a school in an area close to Oys Local Government area without knowing it. I had requested to ease myself on a lonely bush next to what looked like an abandoned farm house. I really had to do this since I may not run into a lavatory anytime soon. The building looked deserted, and I really was afraid of snakes, or other dangerous reptiles.

I thought I heard a sound, and I was right. A bunch of kids were rushing out from another end of the shanty building – and it turned out this was a primary school, and these kids were actually rushing out for a recess. A primary school? Yes! I took a tour and cried again for our continent; our nation; our leaders, and our children. It was a ramshackle building with only two notable structures: dilapidated walls and rusted roofless zinc top. The zincs were riddled with holes, and the wall windows were all fallen apart. The walls revealed an original brick slab and repulsive patches of clay and cement riddled with holes and dirt; same wall were being used as blackboards and one could notice cracks and distractive holes in-between lessons written in white chalk. Seats and desks were some horrible constructed wooden structures, long enough to hold as many pupils – with nails sticking out from various spots.

I am not talking about Guantanamo Bay detention camp – I am describing a primary school here; supposedly, a domain designed for the teaching of our kids. The little field in front of the school was overgrown with weeds, but blessed with two wooden soccer goal posts. Funny enough, kids were happy, jumping around and playing soccer, while some others played other games. Poor kids! They did not understand why they had to get education under such agonizing disaster - besides, they may not have seen any other school besides their structured shanty houses.

I wasn't actually being nosey, wandering around a neighborhood primary school uninvited; but I'm on a mission, a see-it-yourself mission that offers me a more authentic source of information; some pieces that may not be available in Google, and it paid off because I saw them with my own eyes.

Yet the story of a neglected education sector in Nigeria remains another apologetic tale. For instance, it would cost less than $5,000 (UDS) to restructure this institution with decent

■ These are **Kids Learning**. The shocking revelation about every major local government in this country, especially in the south is that there is so much money in the system, thousands of development contracts exchange hands; there are budgets and large money expenditures, yet nothing gets done. *Photo: nairaland.com.*

buildings, fence, reading and teaching accessories, and bathrooms. But an average local government chairman or even a town representative thrives in prosperity; operates local and international bank accounts with funds stolen from tax payers.

In 2004, a Houston escort (prostitute), called Nancy (her real name) told me about her supposedly "friend with benefits" that comes regularly all the way from Abuna, Nigeria's capital

STATE of NIGERIAN SCHOOLS

■ Generally, no single state or region in Nigeria is exonerated from operating a rundown education system. Most public secondary schools in Nigeria look like Nazi concentration camps; the only difference being that the former is a school and the latter is a torture detention camp. But these states, and indeed the nation have enough money to fix this catastrophe.

PHOTOS:

■ Pages **51-52:** *Caroline Knowles 2011 assessment tour, 2011* - The international volunteer wrote, "Some of the schools were quite remote. This school was far from the main road and down a very bumpy track. As you can see it is in a very bad state. The roof is falling in and there is little furniture. The classrooms are very depressing and the blackboard is full of holes making it difficult to write on."

■ Page **53:** *Faith Abiodun, founder & President of The F.A.I.T.H.* Abiodun wrote, "We have failed to provide them with conducive learning environments, experienced and dedicated teachers, comprehensive learning materials, valuable teaching facilities, adequate attention and non-negotiable extra-curricular activities."

city. It turned out to be a senator, and in fact a member of the House Committee on Petroleum Resources. Nancy received more than $3,000 (USD) from her man, and had also made several trips to Nigeria on his behalf. The irony, however, is that the honorable senator has no decent primary school in his constituency.

Generally, no single state or region in Nigeria is exonerated from operating a rundown education system. Most public secondary schools in Nigeria look like Nazi concentration camps; the only difference being that the former is a school and the latter is a torture detention camp. But these states, and indeed the nation have enough money to fix this catastrophe.

By the way, have we forgotten that most public officers absconded with millions of Dollars after they leave office? The former governor of Delta State, for instance Chief James Onanefe Ibori, (See mug shot on page 44) who stood trial for corruption and money laundering charges in a UK court, (case number T20117192) was jailed in April 2012 for 13 years, having pleaded guilty to a 10-count charge of fraud, money laundering and corruption estimated about $250 million. For goodness sake this money can revamp the entire education system in his state and bless citizens with decent schools and tutorial culture.

In the mid eighties, some states embarked on some kind of urban renewal plans aimed at upgrading the environment of slum communities by building roads and drainage channels and providing water supply, electricity, schools and health clinics. At the moment, the fallacies in such bogus projects have come to surface, leaving this West African region with a hopelessly high rate of structural underdevelopment and economic insecurity.

I talked to a journalist in Awka, the capital of Anambra State in the East, and he was so excited that the incumbent Governor did a good job with a few major roads. He referred me to a road connecting Nteje and Aguleri which I also visited. It turned out to be another disappointment; an eye-sore of a road construction standard, signifying the dysfunctional nature of capital management in this region. Smooth-looking road, but at a closer look unveiled a mixture of dirty sand and coal-tar surface. The road edges are rough and untreated and already being washed away by flood water, and pot holes are beginning to develop.

This is typically some form of road construction fraud prevalent in this country. Top officials of the government agencies fraudulently share funds allotted for projects with contractors through kick-backs or bribery. Therefore, by the time the contract is actually awarded, little or nothing is left to execute a quality job. This is why most Nigerian roads do not survive beyond two rainy seasons before wearing off.

Institute of Transportation Studies of University of California, emphasized in a technology transfer program, major fundamentals of a good road project. Three rudiments stood out from a list of ten mandatory tips; keeping water away from the road, building for traffic loads and traffic volumes, and emphasis on road protection and maintenance.

Effective drainage system means everything in road construction and maintenance. Flooding or any water consequence could impede road serviceability. Flood water may cripple the base and weaken the road surface - thus opening up potholes and cracks. Consequently, roads are designed to hold the largest volume of users under normal operations. A good estimation of traffic loads and traffic volumes must be put into consideration in road project development process. The more roads are exposed to adverse weather conditions, bigger weight and regu-

■ **This is a road**: the Asaba-Onitsha Road Expressway was a disappointment. There is typically some form of road construction fraud prevalent in this country. Top officials of the government agencies fraudulently share funds allotted for projects with contractors through kick-backs or bribery. Thus, by the time the contract is actually awarded, little or nothing is left to execute a quality job. *Photo: nigeriainfrastructure.*

larity of traffic, the more chances of deterioration; but a good maintenance strategy complements durability, and saves unusual rehabilitation budget. Maintenance activities must entail treatment of roadway surfaces, including patching, and resurfacing; drainage, cleaning, and repairing culverts and ditches; and applicable traffic services such as sign maintenance; cutting vegetation to maintain visibility.

In Nigeria, the local and state governments are not the only culprits in denying their constituents basic amenities; the central government seriously lags behind in her own responsibility in providing good road network, especially in the area of maintenance, and creating more accessible roads through the hinterlands. As of my visit in 2006, the busiest roads in the country remained a death trap for lack of maintenance, claiming hundreds of lives annually in motor accidents. *Shagamu-Ore-Benin* Expressway, *Iwo-Osogbo* Expressway, *Lagos-Ibadan* Expressway, *Lagos-Badagry* Expressway, *Ibadan-Ilorin* Expressway, *Calabar-Uyo* Expressway, *Aba* Expressway among others remained in deplorable condition. At *Enugu-Awka-Onitsha* road, the busiest in the east, a shabby maintenance contract executed with cheap sand and coal-tar, and without any irrigation structures left travelers on the dual carriage way in harm's way, as such projects hardly survive any season.

It was most interesting to note that Nigeria actually has a ministry that overseas air transportation. The Federal Ministry of Aviation has overall responsibility for the formulation and management of Government's aviation policies in Nigeria. It is empowered under the Nigeria Civil Aviation Act of 1964 to make policies and regulate air navigation. Furthermore, this Ministry is directly responsible for overseeing air transportation, airport development and maintenance, provision of aviation infrastructure services and other needs arising from a wide spectrum in the aviation industry both nationally and globally.

But my experience with air transportation in my 2006 trip opens up another can of creepy worms. After visiting just two local airports, and after interviewing a key high-ranking aviation official who pleaded for anonymity, I fasted for three hours, called my Parish Priest and prayed with him before I boarded a local plane called Aero for a 50-minute flight to the Coal City, Enugu. After more than four major air disasters that have descended on this country within 24 months of this period, [1] observers had thought that casualties and other repercussions would have awakened a sleeping incumbent regime under

■ This is not a local café meal menu board: it is actually a flight information board at a local **Airport** in the Coal City called Enugu. I didn't know I
was at the airport. I thought I was in a Hispanic flee market. The folks I
thought were resale clerks turned out to be booking and other counter
agents. They would smile at you, and first of all say you don't have a
reservation. Don't even argue, because all they need is bribe money and
you are cleared.

(1) Page 57. Major air catastrophes in the Nigerian between 2005 and 2006;
■ **October 22, 2005:** Boeing 737 belonging to *Bellview Airlines* with 117 people
   on board crashed shortly after take-off from Lagos killing all on board.
■ **December 10, 2005:** A *Sosoliso Airlines* DC-9 crashd in Port Harcourt, killing
   all 103 on board.
■ **September 17, 2006:** Only three survived when an 18-seater Dornier 228
   Nigerian Air Force transport plane, carrying 15 senior army officers and three
   crew members crashed in Benue State, Nigeria.
■ **October 29, 2006:** A Boeing 737 Airline with 104 on board belonging to *Aviation Development Corporation* crashed minutes after take-off from Abuja's airport. All but 6 perished in the disaster.

whose leadership the aviation industry went into a deadly slumber. But no!

Enugu Airport…? I didn't know I was at the airport. I thought I was in a Hispanic flee market. The folks I thought were resale clerks turned out to be booking and other counter agents. They would smile at you at first, then say you don't have a reservation. Don't even argue, because all they need is bribe money, and you are cleared. What about the hand luggage scanners? They may or may not be working, but I sure did not hear a single beep, even when I had all sorts of liquid in my hand luggage.

At present, the same ramshackle aviation industry is still plagued by corruption and suffers deadly negligence. Though some popular airlines were grounded for standard violation, a member of a panel assigned to evaluate issues with the industry and fashion out solutions confided to me that, as of date, their studies and recommendations were yet to be enforced by the authorities.

Local airports lack adequate aviation and safety equipment. An assessment of just two local airports left me open-mouthed. Airports gates are not installed and passengers have to walk into the runways to first, identify their luggage, and then board their flights through a wobbly mobile boarding staircase. Airport screening equipment was obsolete and, in fact, could not detect liquids, toothpastes, and sharp shaving objects in my hand luggage. Worse, to my surprise, a security officer cleared my other bags without any check, then turned around and asked me for a tip! Thank God I wasn't a terrorist - This country would have been counting dead bodies.

But these events are really discouraging for such a country where most politicians are far richer than the public coffer. Air

■ File photos of **typical boarding scenes on dilapidated runways.** At present, the same ramshackle aviation industry is still plagued by corruption and suffers deadly negligence. Local airports lack adequate aviation and safety equipment. An assessment of just two local airports left me open-mouthed. Airports gates are not installed and passengers have to walk into the runways to first, identify their luggage, and then board their flights through a wobbly mobile boarding staircase.

safety is a necessity in any growing economy. Remember this was in 2006, when a rapid growth in global air transportation prompted large and small airports to develop and expand their infrastructures. Amidst a prevailing global war on terror, people and baggage handling were often prioritized to ensure safety and reliability, and to overcome longer distances in shorter times. This was why integrated and modern high-speed baggage handling systems were needed to pragmatically impel the proper tracking and movement of luggage and parcels.

It was shocking at the time to observe that conveyor and process belts at the airports do not work beyond the check-in counters. At the Enugu Airport for instance, loaders had to manually haul all luggage beside the aircraft and passengers were made to identify their belongings before they were loaded into the aircraft. Belt loaders are vehicles with movable belts for unloading and loading of baggage and cargo of aircraft. This device is positioned to the door ridge of an aircraft hold or baggage compartment for easy function.

Most disappointing was that baggage carts often used for the transportation of luggage, mail, cargo and other materials between the aircraft and the terminal or sorting facility were conspicuously lacking; even the cheapest trolleys for containers and pallets often used for the transport of loads placed in containers and on pallets were nowhere to be found.

The issue is that all these ground support equipment constitute airport safety. For instance, the aircraft boarding staircase was designed for the safe and efficient boarding and de-boarding of narrow and wide bodied aircraft. This is essential for an aircraft to allow a safe and smooth entry for passengers going in and out of the aircraft. Boarding stairs are mobile and can be rolled into place when the aircraft is on the ground.

■ I had predicted more shocking air disasters if the government kept ignoring an upgrade of their air transport system. Almost six years later,
2012, Nigeria again made global news with another deadly crash. A
Dana plane crashed into a heavily populated area, Iju Agege, Lagos on
a horrible Sunday evening, June, killing everyone on board.
Photo by *Daily Mail:* Onlookers survey the rubble and remains of the
crash.

However the one I saw at this airport, which I also boarded,
gave me another food for thought. It was a raggedy stair scrap
manually pulled by hefty-looking dudes. My mind quickly went
to Houston's Hobby Airport; a local airport just like Enugu Airport where I was still standing in a sluggishly moving line, on
the runway approaching this dilapidated boarding staircase.

Hobby is really nothing to write home about compared to
most local airports in United States; yet it is well equipped and
managed by humans. Powered equipment on the ground shows
a different scenario; a sharp contrast from my current predicament in Enugu. Again, I missed Texas where airports are
blessed with Aircraft re-fuelers cruising in self contained fuel
or hydrant trucks; I taught about those ground power units or
vehicles supplying power to aircraft parked on the ground; I re-

membered those power belt loaders loading and unloading baggage and cargo of aircraft; or even power pullback tugs that pushes an aircraft away from the gate when it is ready to leave. God, I said to myself, mismanagement is really an incurable disease.

I recall when I came back from my Nigerian trip in 2006 and was confronted by a few Nigerian self-acclaimed patriots who thought I was unpatriotic to render a true account of my journey; I reminded them about my chat with a member of a panel assigned to evaluate the country's air industry who confided to me that their studies and recommendations were ignored by the same government who appointed them to that duty. I predicted more shocking air disasters if the government kept ignoring an upgrade of their air transport system. Almost six years later, 2012, Nigeria again made global news with another deadly crash. A Dana plane crashed into a heavily populated area, Iju Agege, Lagos on a horrible Sunday evening, June, killing everyone on board.

The irony of this whole disorder is that Nigeria, an OPEC staunch member and one of the world's largest oil exporters cannot even provide fuel to its people. Nigeria is a major oil supplier to Western Europe and remains the 5th largest supplier of crude oil to the United States. Ironically, I witnessed during my visit in 2006 how motorists scramble for fuel. In some cities, it's like waiting for a visa interview at the United States Embassy in Lagos. You can see a long queue of people and cars, but may neither see the beginning nor the end.

Fuel scarcity hits this region consistently, making mobility difficult. December of 2005, the region suffered serious fuel scarcity that crippled movement around the country, frustrating holiday-makers who had to travel for Christmas. As of late January 2006, motorists were still spending endless hours at gas stations trying to get fuel. In the heat of this calamity, Mr. Funso Kupolokun, then Group Managing Director of Nigerian National Petroleum Corporation (NNPC) at the time admitted that the country depended 100 percent on imported refined petroleum products for its fuel needs. In fact, since 2003, this country has been running on 100 percent imported fuels, but the government at the time headed by Olusegun Obasanjo misled the nation into believing it was importing only 28 percent of its domestic fuel needs.

According to reports at that time, the 125,000 barrel-a-day (bpd) Warri refinery and the 110,000 bpd Kaduna plant were closed after militants, fighting for local control of the Niger Delta's oil wealth blew up the main feeder pipeline. The 210,000 bpd Port Harcourt plant was also shut down due to technical problems. Yet, the central government often downplays the escalating political and ethnic strife in the Niger Delta region, including violence, kidnapping, sabotage, and the seizure of oil facilities, which often disrupt Nigeria's oil production.

It may be recalled that on March 19, 2003, Chevron Texaco suspended its oil production in the Niger Delta region, declaring force majeure on its exports following violent clashes between the Ijaw and the Itsekiri ethnic groups which crippled the operations of the oil companies in the area. That was not all. Shell, another company with facilities in the region, removed its nonessential staff.

Both companies had shut down their operations and evacuated all personnel. Chevron Texaco shut-down production of 140,000 bpd and Shell closed down its flow stations with a combined capacity of 126,000 bpd. The 266,000 bpd of lost oil represented approximately 13 % of Nigeria's total average production. The same month, Shell evacuated four oil facilities, oil pipeline pumping stations at Ogbotobo, Opukushi, Tumo, and Benisede, raising the number of closed Shell facilities to 14.[1]

At the period, conditions in this country clearly riddled with mismanagement and corruption among the ruling class. Revenue allocations were made without accountability, and worse, some rural areas operated without local government while development funds end up in the hands of state officials who channelled them to private banks abroad.

Professor Aluko[2] of Obafemi Awolowo University, Ile-Ife, Nigeria once wrote in one of his dissertations, that when corruption becomes institutionalized in a society, it infiltrates into the value-system, becomes a norm, part and parcel of culture, and subsequently goes into the realm of behavior. Aluko is absolutely right, because the corruption issue in Nigeria has outfashioned any mode of problem evaluation. In fact, as of 2006, it was estimated that more than $10 Billion of what is supposed to be in the government accounts in Nigeria are out in foreign banks, while the masses suffer the repercussions.

As of 2008, most former governors were already facing charges of large money embezzlement. For instance, Boni Haruna who ran northeast Adamawa state for eight years during the term of a former president Olusegun Obasanjo was accused of stealing over $790,000, between 1999 and 2007 tenure. Most disappointedly, the country's state governors controlling millions of dollars of public funds are shielded with immunity from

---

(1) **International Guardian** Energy Report, 2003.
(2) **Aluko, M.** (2002) *The Institutionalization of Corruption and Its Impact On Political Culture and Behavior in Nigeria.*

criminal prosecution while in office.

It may be recalled that James Ibori, a former governor of Delta admitted fraud totaling nearly £50 million, which is said to be part of total embezzlement that exceeded 250 million US dollars. Ibori pleaded guilty February 12, 2012, at Southwark Crown Court to a series of charges linked to the theft of money from the Delta State and fraud involving state-owned shares in a mobile phone firm.

Also, we must bear in mind that Mr. Ibori was working as a cashier in a branch of a DIY store in Ruislip, Middlesex, before he moved to Nigeria and worked his way up through the political ranks to become a state governor in 1999. The *Telegraph* reported how as governor of the state, he was racking up credit card bills of 200,000 US dollars per month on a luxury lifestyle, including running a fleet of armored Range Rovers. Funny enough, Ibori was trying to buy a plane for £20 million at the time he was arrested. His wife Theresa Ibori, sister Christine Ibori-Idie, mistress Udoamaka Okoronkwo, and a London-based solicitor, Bhadresh Gohil were already convicted of money-laundering.

Professor Aluko, insisted that Nigeria has long been treading the brink of this national catastrophe due to the almost uncontainable intensity of corruption of a viable, virile, and stable polity, which also constitutes the greatest hindrance to the moral uprightness of the citizens.

6

The Fallacy of One Nigeria: The Psychology of "To Live or Not to Live"

■ Founding Fathers and Tribal Leaders are definitely not the same. Those who made significant intellectual contributions to the constitution of the land, or fight selflessly for attainment of nationhood could pass for the "Founding Fathers" of a country. Major issue with early Nigerian political scholars is being unable to distinguish between Founding Fathers and Tribal Leaders.

The psychological theory of "to live or not to live" is best attributed to Shakespeare's legendary play (1602); one of his most fascinating philosophical phrases from his work "Hamlet." "To be, or not to be: that is the question" is a line out of a long composition of strong words spoken by Hamlet (character) as he contemplated suicide. For him, the major issue was whether to continue to exist or not – whether it was more dignified to suffer the wraths of the prevalent excruciating circumstances, or to bare fangs and confront them.

This Shakespeare's work has since soared, and created a founda-

■ Foreground: **Abubakar Tafawa Balewa** became Nigeria's Prime Minister; **Sultan of Sokoto, Sir Ahmadu Bello** (background) was first Premier of the Northern Nigeria region from 1954-1966. Unfortunately, The Sultan, a decorated founding father was also a leading opposition to Nigeria's attainment of independence, in 1960.

tion to philosophical exploration of life and death, as well as divine option and connectivity for coexistence. Contemporary writers, authors, and political philosophers also interpreted Shakespeare's work from various perspectives. For instance, former Israeli Leader, Golda Meir (1898- 1978) said that "To be or not to be is not a question of compromise. Either you be or you don't be;" Contemporary American Author, Tom Robbins, wrote that "To be or not to be isn't the question. The question is how to prolong being;" Contemporary American novelist, Chuck Palahniuk, believed that "You have a choice. Live or die. Every breath is a choice. Every minute is a choice."

Great thinkers in history also made a sense of thoughts similar to this phrase: Greek Philosopher, Aristotle charged that "No one would choose a friendless existence on condition of having all the other things in the world." German Philosopher, Nietzsche stated that "Existence really is an imperfect tense that never becomes a present" and finally, American Psychologist, Fromm (1900-1980) assumed that "Man is the only animal for whom his own existence is a problem which he has to solved."

There is, however, one major thing that these commentators and philosophers did not realize about this metaphorical question of "To be, or not to be:" They had no slightest idea that Shakespeare was actually predicting issues in Nigeria, Africa's most populous country, when he wrote this phrase. From the creation of this nation as a British Colony, coexistence between the North and South has remained a miscalculated experiment effected with the wrong apparatuses – thus making a peaceful existence as a nation impracticable. The North was nurtured under intolerant Islamist religious doctrine, whereas the South retained their traditional heritage and embraced western civilization, including Christianity. Besides the conflicting governance nature of indirect rule applied by the British colonialists,

■ **Sir Frederick Lugard**, was first Governor general of Nigeria Colonialism (1914- 1919).
From the creation of this nation by the British, coexistence between the North and South has remained a misjudged experiment effected with the wrong apparatuses – thus making a peaceful existence as a nation impracticable

the marriage of these regions and introduction of democracy without a strategic reconciliation of tribal, cultural, and religious issues are like building a sand dome in the Galveston beach with 70% chances of thunderstorm.

The basic culture of a "Democratic governance moves beyond the mere procedure of democracy and the establishment of democratic institutions," concluded a United Nations Integrated Mission in Timor-Leste... "it involves promoting the retention of democracy which includes an enduring capacity for: the separation of powers and independence of the branches of government; the exercise of power in accordance with the rule of law; the respect for human rights and fundamental freedoms; and, the transparency and accountability of a responsible civil service, functioning at both the national and local levels."[1]

Views, however by Koenig and de Guchteneire [2] on political governance of cultural diversity rightly added that "The challenge for democracies" is to design policies that explicitly recognize cultural differences, while ensuring inclusion and furthering the common bonds and sense of solidarity that are necessary for the functioning of democratic society." Koenig and de Guchteneire[3] questioned how the recognition of cultural differences is reconciled with the social reproduction of trust and solidarity that is necessary for the maintenance of a democratic polity? The second dilemma, according to Koenig and de Guchteneire [4] is how to reconcile the recognition of minorities as groups with the concept of human rights, which focuses on the rights of the individual person. Put differently, how can constitutional arrangements mediate between different

---

(1) **United Nations Integrated Mission in Timor-Leste** (2012) *Democratic Governance; What is democratic Governance?*
(2-4) **Koenig, M & de Guchteneire, P.** (2007) Political Governance of Cultural Diversity. Democracy and Human Rights in Multicultural Societies. Intro.pdf

groups' collective rights of self-rule and the individual's rights to inclusion in the larger polity?[1]

Such contradiction in application of democracy in a multi-cultural organizations, and political governance of cultural diversity accounted to why Nigeria's nationhood may have remained threatened by North and South dichotomy and sectarian violence, amidst the worse governance culture and structure in the history of political science. Till date, senseless mutilations of humans in the North occur in great numbers. Just recently, an Islamic militant group in the North claimed responsibility for attacks that killed at least 25 people in a rash of violence against the country's minority Christians; this was after it issued an earlier ultimatum that gave Christians three days to leave the area.[1] In its normal fashion, a deadly violence between Christians and Muslims in Nigeria's Kaduna flared again, adding more deaths in sectarian clashes[2].

Before I begin to explain the coloration between these killings, and the mythical notion of "One Nation-One-Destiny," a misleading slogan often used by the ruling class to cover-up piercing religious, cultural, and tribal issues, I must respectfully warn that Nigerians intoxicated by this dogma, and who detest discussing critical issues in "Black and White" should please stay away from this chapter - for this may not be a Jerry Springer[3] affair!

From its independence in 1960 till date, cost of the insurgency in Nigeria has at least been consistent with little or no mitigating strategy by the leadership class. But the recent lethal advances of killings in the North remain a shocking experience: for instance, between July 2009 and March 2012, the Boko Haram had conducted roughly

---

(1) **CNN,** January 12, 2012).
(2) **Reuters,** (June 20, 2012). Sectarian violence kills more in Nigeria's Kaduna http://af.reuters.com/
(3) **Norman "Jerry" Springer:** British-born American television presenter, best known as host of the tabloid talk show, "Jerry Springer."

170 separate attacks, with thousands of deaths and casualties. The sect has concentrated its attacks mainly in Northern Nigeria, including this threat on January 2012, asking Southerners and Christians to leave the North within three days.

Drafting a problem statement—a statement of purpose by different studies initiated to seek a long-term solution has never been lacking. Political science scholar, Dr. Aliyu Odamah Musa [1] in the *Journal of African Media Studies* unleashed this problem statement that could dovetail any investigational research reality;

> "Between 18 and 19 December 1980 a radical Islamist group unleashed a major mayhem in the commercial city of Kano. In the violence at least 5000 lives were lost (Falola 1998) and property worth several millions of dollars was destroyed. The group, named Maitatsine after its founder Muhammadu Marwa Maitatsine, laid the foundation for a series of violent religious disturbances in Northern Nigeria, including many it directly fuelled."

Whereas analysts and observers are all in agreement about the Northern Muslim genocide of Christians, mainly from the South, conclusions, solutions, and underlying philosophies remain a multicolor display. For instance, in his conclusive revelation, Dr. Musa gave an 8-point postulation that questions the scholarliness of his dissertation. His words read;

Finally, this article postulates that:

> "(1) the main motivation of Boko Haram is economic and not religious;
>
> (2) the Boko Haram monster is not invincible and can be tamed;
>
> (3) its main strategy is to incite people against others in

---

(1) **Musa, A.** (2012). Socio-economic incentives, news media and the Boko Haram campaign of violence in Northern Nigeria. *Journal of African Media Studies.*

order to achieve its ulterior motive;

(4) the al-majirai, street children, have been identified as highly vulnerable and easy to manipulate and are therefore targeted, recruited and used as foot soldiers;

(5) technology, which they denounce, is a major asset to their activities;

(6) despite not having proper western education they are able to make and use deadly explosives;

(7) although the source of Boko Haram funding has not been fully unraveled there are suggestions that they get financial support from people secretly affiliated to them; and

(8) given an assurance for a genuine dialogue, the group might agree to take part and even drop its demand for Sharia law." [1]

Dr. Musa started with a sound issue scrutiny but flawed the truth-seeking bearing of his purpose with the most fallacious supposition that wrongly attributed the motivation of Boko Haram to economic hardship rather than religious fanaticism. The most misleading assumptions are those that either fuse Boko Haram's lethal advances to prevalent austerity in Nigeria, or those that play down their Islamic beliefs and practice.

Boko Haram today thrives more of their radical beliefs. The members are smart, ruthless, schooled in their beliefs regarding non-Muslims, and western education. According to the Institute for the Study of Violent Groups, Boko Haram are spread out from Nigeria,

---

(1) **Musa, A.** (2012). Socio-economic incentives, news media and the Boko Haram campaign of violence in Northern Nigeria. *Journal Of African Media Studies.*

through Chad, Cameroon, Mali, and Somalia.[1]

A recent United States and North Atlantic Treaty Organization (NATO) reports indicated that the North African group Al-Qaeda in the Islamic Maghreb (AQIM) and the Somali militant group Al-Shabaab have been able to establish not only religious and ideological ties to Boko Haram, but also have been able to provide them with training and financial support.

It is also a fact that, from "Maitatsine" to "Boko Haram," Islamic fundamentalism and sectarian violence in Northern Nigeria have been discharging some hypothetical certainty. Besides a long list of organizational credence among these killer-groups, the uniformity in ideology points to a single condition: Islamization of Nigeria – therefore, let's start our discussion by invoking some great quotes of the past that may validate the notion that Nigeria was never meant to be.

Abubakar Tafawa Balewa considered one of the founding fathers, who later became Nigeria's Prime Minister, in his address to the Northern House of Assembly in 1952 shocked the nation when he said;

> "The Southern people who are swamping into this region daily in such large numbers are really intruders. We don't want them and they are not welcome here in the North. Since 1914 the British Government has been trying to make Nigeria into one country. But the people are different in every way, including religion, custom, language and aspirations…We in the North take it that Nigeria's unity is only a British intention for the country they created. It is not for us"[2]

Consequently, the Sultan of Sokoto, Sir Ahmadu Bello, first pre-

---

(1) **Study of Violent Groups © 2012.**
(2) Adapted from **International Guardian** documentary, 2003.

mier of the Northern Nigeria region (1954-1966), also considered one of the founding fathers, was a leading opposition to Nigeria's attainment of independence, in October 12, 1960. The Sultan had this to say a few days after Nigeria finally regained self-resurgence from the British Colony:

> "The new nation called Nigeria should be an estate from our great-grandfather Othoman Dan Fodio. We must ruthlessly prevent a change of power. We must use the minorities in the North as willing tools, and the South as conquered territories and never allow them to have control of their future."[1]

The Sultan we all know, is the son of a district head and heir to the Sokoto Caliphate; his great-grandfather was Sultan Bello, the founder of Sokoto and son of the revered Shaykh Usman Dan Fodio.

Realistically, it must be noted, in Nigeria's context, that founding fathers and tribal leaders are definitely not the same. Those who made significant intellectual contributions to the constitution of the land, or fight selflessly for attainment of nationhood could pass for the "Founding Fathers" of a country. Major issue with early Nigerian political scholars is being unable to distinguish between founding fathers and tribal leaders.

Remember that name - Shehu Usman Dan Fodio? Usman Dan Fodio,[2] (born December 1754, Maratta, Gobir, Hausaland [now in Nigeria]—died 1817, Sokoto, Fulani empire), is a Fulani mystic, philosopher, and revolutionary reformer who, in a jihad (holy war) between 1804 and 1808, created a new Muslim state, the Fulani Empire, in what is now Northern Nigeria.

It may be recalled that when Usman Dan Fodio declared the Jihad in 1804, his genuine desire was a firm establishment of Islam in

(1) Adapted from **International Guardian** documentary, 2003.
(2) Definition: **Encyclopedia Britannica**

Hausa land. His punitive religious purpose and radical execution of Jihad are aimed at overthrowing the prevailing mandate to establish the order of Islam.

In his account of the Jihad of Usman Dan Fodio, Ibraheem Sulaiman explained in part, under a sub topic, *"Overthrow of the Decadent Order"*[1] the validity of a struggle between Islam and *kufr* (infidels): maintaining that the ultimate objective of *tajdid* (Arabic word for renewal) was a forceful overthrow of the prevalent order and the establishment of the command of Islam.

Usman Dan Fodio's doctrine, according to Sulaiman was that, *"Kufr* had had its days, decades and centuries, now it was the turn of Islam, the turn of faith, truth, liberty and justice." Dan Fodio, thus reiterated his conditions for determining the legal status of a country with the philosophical validation, that "If the ruler is a Muslim then the country is Muslim, if he is an unbeliever, then the country is one of unbelief."

Dan Fodio's cause was a struggle against specific governance paradigms, categorized under four unacceptable standards. The first was government established by unbelievers. Such governments, in Hausa land, regarded as pagans, must suffer being swept from power by a militant revolution. The second was a regime whose rulers were "…unbelievers in their hearts who, through political expedience had to manifest Islam and associate with Muslims."[2] The third was a government whose leaders had committed treason by coming to power in the name of Islam and then abandoning Islam when fully established.[3] The fourth was government of syncretic rulers who governed in the name of Islam but whose policies and strategies were based on secular objectives, principles, and institutions.[4]

(1-4) **Sulaiman I** (1982) *A Revolution in History: The Jihad of Usman Dan Fodio.*

Dan Fodio's orders to the people of Bilad al-Sudan,[1] tagged "obligatory by consensus", therefore became a non-negotiable spiritual commitments, namely:

1. To fight against an unbelieving king who has never in his life declared "There is no deity but Allah, and to take the reins of government from him."

2. To fight against an unbelieving king who declares "There is no deity but Allah for the mere purpose of satisfying the established custom of the country, but who in reality does not profess Islam, and to take the reins of government from him."

3. To fight against an apostate king who abandons Islam and reverts to unbelief, and to take the reins of government from him.

4. To fight against an apostate king who outwardly remains within the fold of Islam but who, nevertheless, syncretizes the practices of Islam with the practices of unbelief (like most of the Hausa kings), and to take the reins of government from him.[2]

Coming at a period Muslims around the globe were working to widen Islamic doctrines as possible antidote to a growing religious and socio-cultural improbability, Sulaiman not only unraveled the philosophical application of the fanatic order of Shehu Usman Dan Fodio, but also made a significant declaration that his work will help define the future of Muslims. For indeed, he wrote, "A people without a history, are a people without a future. At this critical point one hopes and prays that Muslims will not betray their history - should

---

(1) *"Bilad al Sudan"* was the name given by medieval Muslims to the belt of African territory south of the Sahara Desert and extending from the Atlantic to the Ethiopian plateau.
(2) **Sulaiman I** (1982) *A Revolution in History: The Jihad of Usman Dan Fodio.*

they do so, history will certainly betray them."

Therefore, I maintain without any more details, that Sir Ahmadu Bello, a descendant of Othoman Dan Fodio, understood unequivocally, the mechanics of his religious history and ideology, when he declared in October 12, 1960, the month of Nigeria's independence that "The new nation called Nigeria should be an estate from our great-grandfather Othoman Dan Fodio."

Today, this period in 2013, the Hausa Land, now called Northern Nigeria has punitively, while undermining the secularity of Nigeria's nationhood, operated all the major Islamic standards as applies to the radical institution of their spiritual founding fathers. The Islamization of Nigeria's currency (Naira and Kobo); movement of Nigeria's capital city from west to the North; establishment of Sharia Court; forceful induction of Nigeria into the Organization of Islamic Conference; introduction of Islamic Banking; monopoly of political and economic powers, and so on are clear indication that the existence of Nigeria as a nation is a fraudulent conjecture that bear no theoretical relevance.

The philosophical revelation is that the country called Nigeria was crafted on a wrong path; the ideological gap between the North and South was not objectively addressed by the British Colonial masters before a manipulated census that led to formulation of the first republic. Wrote Adebola Adeoye,[1] *(The African Currier)* on Nigeria about the same issue;

> "To manipulate future power relations in a post-independent Nigeria meant the population of the country must be skewed in favor of the North to guarantee that the Northerners would have more electoral representation in the fed-

---

(1) **Adeoye, A.** (2010) How the British planted the seed of disunity in Nigeria - *The African Courier.*

eral legislature that is disproportional to their true demographic size. That was exactly what the British did in the first official census conducted in Nigeria in 1952/53 by massively rigging the head count in favor of the North. That census showed that inhabitants of the North constituted 55.4 per cent of Nigeria's population of 30.42 million. All incidental indicators of population, however, showed that the South should be more populous."

Dr. Francois Duvalier, President of The Republic of Haiti, echoed a similar sentiment in his infamous letter to the British Prime Minister, March 22 1969. Dr. Duvalier wrote about the authenticity of Nigeria's nationhood;

"A left-over of colonialism which worked relentlessly at destroying the structures of Negro-African civilizations and demarcating boundaries with her own interests as the sole criterion; Federal Nigeria has never since her independence shown the distinctive mark of a united nation. It has been impossible for her to silence tribal rivalries - to achieve the mixture of ethnic and cultures likely to secure national unity."

There is every indication that the components of Nigeria's secularity exists only in part of her written constitution but bears no similitude to practicality. For instance, shortly before the polls that saw a lawful election of the first minority president, Goodluck Jonathan, Alhaji Lawan Kaita, a founding member of the ruling People's Democratic Party (PDP), and a close ally of a Northern candidate Atiku Abubakar, warned that the North should not be blamed for the calamity that will befall the country, if Jonathan emerges President. He vowed;

"We will continue to wage war against the Nigerian state until we abolish the secular system and establish an Islamic state. The North is determined, if that happens, to make the country ungovernable for President Jonathan or any other southerner who finds his way to the seat of power on the platform of the PDP against the principle of the party's zoning policy" *(International Guardian).*

Furthermore, it is a fact that Nigeria has been a member of the Organization of The Islamic Conference (OIC) since 1986, questioning its legitimacy as a secular state. Now, do we see where former Libyan leader Muammar Gaddafi[1] was coming from when he suggested that Nigeria should be divided? It may be recalled also, that then military president, Ibrahim Babangida upgraded Nigeria's role in the Organization from a mere observer-status to full-fledged membership, despite the fact that both demography and constitution contradicted his actions. After public outcry, the John Shagaya panel was instituted to determine Nigeria's status in the OIC, subsequently confirming membership and making a recommendation for withdrawal from the body. Till date, this proposed change was never made – leaving Nigeria with more or less an Islamic identity. In other words, it is right to call this nation, the "Islamic Republic of Nigeria;" why not?

Has any Nigerian really questioned why Nigeria's capital city was moved from *Lagos (West)* to *Abuja (North)?* There was this argument, a totally blind argument that Abuja is in the center of Nigeria. That again is illogical. The major reason was clear - a calculated attempt to shove the political and economic power to the North to secure the leadership for the northern oligarchs. If Nigeria must maintain her secularity under one constitution, why are *Sharia laws* fully operational in the North?

While Nigeria, and in deed Nigerians promote this scam called "One Nigeria" please be informed that some crucial OIC's objectives

---

(1) **BBC** (Tuesday, 16 March 2010) Divide Nigeria in two, says Muammar Gaddafi.

and principles which are also binding to Nigeria as a country contravenes every tenet of democratic setting. For instance, Article 1(8-9) of the OIC Charter urges members to support and empower the Palestinian people to exercise their right to self-determination. The Articles read in part;[1]

> **8**. *To support and empower the Palestinian people to exercise their right to self-determination and establish their sovereign State with Al-Quds Al-Sharif as its capital...*
> **9**. *To strengthen intra-Islamic economic and trade cooperation; in order to achieve economic integration leading to the establishment of an Islamic Common Market.*"

So why must Nigeria remain 'one' under such manipulation of democracy and brutal rape of her secularity? Nigeria could start rethinking a complete dialogue on whether to exist as a Nation or not. May I also advise that those who have not really been directly affected by the menace called 'One Nigeria' must speak with some respect and intelligibility, and also seek other sources besides the Google search to update their knowledge on this subject.

It is only those who personally have not experienced the mortal ramifications of this nation that would keep invoking other regional occurrences to cover-up a creative error conceived by the colonialists – a fatal experiment that has produced more misery than harmony; more Christian deaths than holocaust, and worse, more wreckage than the tsunami.

The issue about Nigeria's nationhood is not about love for a failed Nation, and it is not about the power of reconciliation and restoration. It is about the ravages of sacrificing the bloods, goods and chattels of Easterners, Southerners, and Christians to achieve a superficial love that does not exist.

(1) **Charter of the Organization of the Islamic Conference (2006)** Organization of the Islamic Conference.

7

Organizational Design Blackout: A Critical Discussion

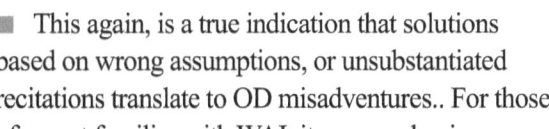

■ This again, is a true indication that solutions based on wrong assumptions, or unsubstantiated recitations translate to OD misadventures.. For those of us not familiar with WAI, it was an abusive program initiated by dictators, Buhari and Idiagbon in the early 80s to "Talibanize" Nigeria.

"The growth and development of people is the highest calling of leadership" (Harvey S. Firestone).

Nigerian-born Nobel Laureate, Professor Wole Soyinka looked at his country very passionately, and declared, "Let's say there are prospects for a new Nigeria, but I don't think we have a new Nigeria yet." Hence, having a new Nigeria means a leadership rebirth to create something new; something that works, and a style of governance that would bring back the confidence of the masses to once again believing in their nation as the only hope for political freedom and economic emancipation.

Another icon and a son of the soil, Professor Chinua Achebe[1] echoed a similar thought attributing Nigeria's woes to a leadership breakdown. Wrote Achebe in his legendary book, *"Trouble with Nigeria;"*

> "The trouble with Nigeria is simply and squarely a failure of leadership. There is nothing basically wrong with the Nigerian character. There is nothing wrong with the Nigerian land or climate or water or air or anything else. The Nigerian problem is the unwillingness or inability of its leaders to rise to the responsibility; to the challenge of personal example which are the hallmarks of true leadership."

I am not done yet - Oye Ogunbadejo[2] in a paper about ethnicity, and corruption in Nigerian politics traced the origin of political fraud to colonialism. The argument made some sense:

> "No sooner did the country attain independence than the areas of dissension surfaced; a situation worsened by the fact that Britain took no major step to create an integrated society. As was common with all colonial powers, the strategy was to 'divide and rule'. By choosing regional and administrative units which coincided with major ethnic groups - Hausa - Fulani in the North, Ibo in the East, and Yoruba in the West, Britain strengthened ethnic identification and consciousness. The struggle for power at the centre exacerbated this phenomenon. Political parties were regionally based, and, in very broad terms, were ethnically homogeneous."

(1) **Achebe, C. (1983)** *The Trouble with Nigeria.* Heinmann Publisher.
(2) **Ogunbadejo, O.** (1979) Conflict Images: Colonial' Legacy, Ethnicity, and Corruption In Nigerian Politics, 1960-1966 *Utafiti*-Vol.4 No.1 July 1979.

Without doubt, the whole issue with Nigeria is leadership — the leaders behind the designs, and execution of the strategies of governance. With hundreds of journals and dissertations scattered in various academic catalogs citing corruption as the underpinning factor of Nigeria's governance woes, it is perhaps imperative to note that solving corruption issue alone cannot ease this predicament. Achebe got it right when he argued again that "Nigeria is what it is because its leaders are not what they should be." So what would leaders be? In a country of more than 150 million citizens, convoluted by years of military dictatorship, how do leaders embrace an innovative paradigm to transformation? Who are these leaders, and what tools are they armed with to manage a needed change?

Organizational design (OD) and management are critical to any long-term transformation process. Building innovation, managing research and development is a vital problem, particularly for a country controlled for years by blood-hungry despots armed with more assault rifles than human brains. Nevertheless, the structural management of a country like Nigeria should center on comprehension and the use of OD tools and application of various techniques to speed and promote needed development. [1]

A three-fold discussion, in this context, details;

   (1) Nigeria's theoretical leadership analysis and the current organizational design strategies,

   (2) a proposed paradigm to create opportunities for its effective management, and

   (3) how any new transformational model could help this country sustain itself and adapt for the future.

There is a correlation between leaders and their constituents as

---

[1] **Jones, G.R.** (2010). *Organizational Theory, Design, and Change* (6th Ed.). Upper Saddle River, NJ: Prentice Hall.

being detrimental to socio-political and economic progress, but establishing such connection requires a thorough evaluation on Nigeria's strengths, weaknesses, opportunities, and threats (SWOT). Assessment in this context explores the internal and external environments of an organization, extracts convenient development strategies based on its strengths, weaknesses, opportunities, and threats.[1] Most scholars would be quick with general analysis of Nigeria's governance paralysis, but it becomes complicated when it gets to proposing a transformational OD paradigm that would consolidate her strength, and transform her weaknesses, and threats into practicable opportunities.

For instance, how does Nigeria benefit from multiple tribes with conflicting cultures often ascribed as her major weakness in creating structural unity and peace? How does this country translate a wider range of corruption that permeates it internal parliamentary structures into a foregone issue to be learned from? How could democracy in Nigeria embrace an operational model that respects the independence of the three governmental arms; executive, legislature, and judiciary? How could true democracy work in a system where the executive has unchallenged control of the judiciary? How can an electoral board strictly under the control of the executive serve the public interest? These and other critical demands are potential research questions overlooked by Nigerian OD scholars, and policy makers.

The whole world knows that the Nigerian leadership has been corrupt – in fact a blind man could see it very clearly; but workable solutions require some prerequisites tied to constructive OD strategies. Just listen to Aluko [1] in his paper, *Institutionalization of Corruption and its Impact on Political Culture and Behavior in Nigeria*. Aluko suggested two major underpinning factors that

---

(1) Ghazinoory, S., Abdi, M., &Azadegan-Mehr, M. (2011).

would be needed to be addressed in other to cleanse the system; first is the problem of 'Poverty' and the second factor focused on bad governance and leadership. Here are a few of Aluko's recommendations;

- Launching of national reorientation programs to educate people on the crucial need to eradicate corruption in politics.
- Curtailing and discouraging the influence of money as a factor in politics.
- Poverty alleviation to inevitably reduce people's vulnerability and susceptibility to corruption.
- Prosecution of corrupt officials.

Above all, concluded Aluko, "The society has the responsibility to educate, mobilize, socialize, enlighten and sensitize its members towards a tradition of honesty, excellence, truth, diligence, integrity, honor, reputation, good name and other moral virtues that will make the society a better place for the people."

These prescriptions are not impracticable, but how could we tie corruption to poverty in a country where most corrupt citizens come from the affluent leadership class? To make it worse, Aluko's ideas came around 2002, a period when the country was governed by a bunch of illiterates who operated without specific visions. Consequently, it is effective practice, to initiate program to educate people on the essential need to eliminate corruption in politics, but how does the system educate them? Past Nigeria's government anti-corruption programs, it may be recalled, ended up as TV commercials and newspaper Ads, creating little or no impact in achieving the very core objectives.

In further discussion on educating people as a way to eradicate

---

(1) **Aluko, M. (2002).** *The Institutionalization of Corruption and Its Impact on Political Culture and Behavior in Nigeria.*

corruption in politics, Aluko endorsed some previous government programs including War Against Indiscipline (WAI) as steps in the right direction. This again, is a true indication that solutions based on wrong assumptions, or unsubstantiated recitations translate to OD misadventures. For those of us not familiar with WAI, it was an abusive program initiated by dictators, Buhari and Idiagbon in the early 80s.

Similar to the Taliban extreme Islamic ideals, WAI was a vigorous punitive enforcement of moral archetypes and a sense of patriotism on the suffering masses. They are laws for wild animals; more of using horse whips to get the people to singing the national anthem and reciting the national pledge. To make it worse, businesses were sacked for not hoisting the national flags; civil servants were brutalized and denied pay checks for inability to recite the national anthem; soldiers armed to their teeth tortured innocent motorists, and often ask them to sing the national anthem at check points. Without doubt, it became clear that these ruthless military leaders at the time were unable to differentiate between human beings and animals.

Now, my problem is how any scholar, or educational institution, could endorse or reference such senseless programs as a correctional measure in organizational reforms. It is despicable in any academic considerations of the OD methodologies, to even propagandize atrocious programs of these despots. It is also unfortunate that these military leaders engaged most academic scholars and used them to arrange fictitious programs and phony researches to give credibility to their disparaging commands.

This is why it is right to indicate that the wounds inflicted in the spinal frame of the country's leadership system is cancerous, and may not just go away overnight. Consequently, it may be impossible to manage Nigeria without a total obliteration of the current perception of leadership styles, or management strategies. Even before any ethical cultural renaissance is applied to the system, as most OD scholars would agree, it may be necessary to embrace with respect, a governance model that suits the nation's secularity; an environment where the three arms of government function independently, to at least implant some coherence in overhauling the system process.

Let me break it down in more unblemished strokes. No OD medicament can thrive in Nigeria if as a secular nation, it touts a full membership of Organization of Islamic Cooperation (OIC) (formerly Organization of the Islamic Conference). OIC is the collective voice of the Muslim world with the mission to safeguard and protect specifically, the interests of the Muslims.

Under a list of OIC's Charter,[1] is a vow to protect and defend the true image, as well as combating defamation of Islam. Therefore, dealing with intricacies of Nigeria being a federation, and an extreme Islamic outmoded values imposed in the North, coupled with various Christian communities in the South are horrendously an OD nightmare.

Nigeria's leadership woes are worse than Gaza. To make it worse, different leaders in the civilian regimes grappled with strategies to suite specific selfish interests rather than benefit their constituencies. Managing any transformational process in a nation is generally a quest that must be targeted toward improving effectiveness at fundamental levels of the government. In face of prevalent global economic challenges, countries, like never before, are meeting head-on with swift changing environments. The task facing leaders therefore are to respond and adjust to such demands.

It may be advisable, however, not to obfuscate strict 'adherence to the law of the land,' with managing people according to 'dictates

---

(1) **Charter of the Organization of the Islamic Conference (2006).** Organization of the Islamic Conference.

of organizational governance.' Leadership and OD have a language dissimilar to the dialect of the constitution. Jones[1] defined organizational change as a transformation process from a present state to projected future state to improve effectiveness; thus an estimated change can only be effective when leaders understand fundamental difficulties and other barriers that must be overcome.

Nigeria's current regime led by Goodluck Jonathan has been commended for specific transformation strategies, including an inclusion of more women and minorities in the leadership process, yet logical analysis still reveals significant strategic OD technical lapses that impede growth. Dazed by surmountable issues created by his predecessors, President Jonathan has been sandwiched in-between defenseless masses and callous political interest groups that financially supported his candidacy in the election that brought him to office. Managing these two major forces are a nightmare.

Realistically, managing the masses is not only a responsibility, but also the core demands of the president's constitutional tasks. On the contrary, prioritizing measures to please lobbyists and pay back political interest groups are cultic vows the President must fulfill to preserve his political career. Loyalty to his political party, and his godfathers over severe policy issues therefore underscore one of President Jonathan's biggest impediments to any pertinent OD strategies. For instance, in the past two or three regimes in Nigeria, most politicians convicted for high public or corporate fraud are in one way or the other connected to the current leadership. With a shaky judiciary almost subjugated by executive arm, law enforcement and prosecution of these fraudsters remain another political fanfare.

In another realistic vindication, it may be recalled that in Octo-

(1) **Jones, G.R.** (2010). Organizational Theory, Design, and Change (6th Ed.). Upper Saddle River, NJ: Prentice Hall.

ber, 2007, outraged Nigerians called for the removal of the Speaker of the House of Representatives, Patricia Etteh, for her alleged involvement in a $5m scam (Also page 163). Three years later, 2010, there was another bizarre fisticuffs over a missing N9bn[1] sum which another Speaker, Dimeji Bankole, claimed he used to procure eight bullet-proof cars for his office. The irony, however, is that these culprits are not in jail houses; they are still connected to the leadership circle, enjoying high-dollar government contracts.

Nigeria needs an effective leader to coordinate its hysterical organizational structure, but achieving this change needs leaders who speak the OD dialect. Kuhn[2] argued that paradigm shift should be seen as a change from one way of thinking to another and not necessarily a pragmatic organizational reshuffle. According to Kuhn, "It is a revolution, a transformation, a sort of metamorphosis. It just does not happen, but rather it is driven by agents of change," hence, a kind of change that would position this leadership to address imminent challenges. Currently, President Jonathan's team is far from this competence. In fact, besides his economic team where he sought competence and genuineness, most, if not all of his other appointees were mere party contractors, party loyalists, lobbyists, and incompetently, lucky obsequious kinsmen.

A nation is like an organization. Development of organization succeeds effectively when values of learning, growth, and change are prioritized.[3] The mechanics of OD is more than just tools and techniques. According to Gallos, it must also radiate fundamental

---

(1) **N: Naira** - Nigerian currency: 1 Naira equals 0.01 US Dollar (rates fluctuate).
(2) **Kuhn, T. S.** (1962). *The Structure of Scientific Revolutions.* Second Edition, Enlarged, the University of Chicago Press, Chicago.
(3) **Gallos, J.V. (2006, 2007).** *Organization development.* An Francisco, CA; Jossey-Bass.

principles that require participation, learning, justice, and equality, effective communication, and information process, mutual obligation, and other factors that would engage people and foster strategic means to solve problems.

To acquire specific goals in organizational development or design of a country means creating entities that would not only respond to but also satisfy human needs. OD artfully fuses process with content in a pursuit for long-term resolutions of typically tough challenges. Effective leadership always has been integral to the OD change paradigm.[1] A good understanding of the governance process enables leaders to identify how organization works; unfortunately, Nigeria turned out to be one of those African nations ruined since its independence by leaders who only understood how assault weapons worked.

Effective administration cuts across organizing people for resourceful labor but also demands managing people, their knowledge, and needs; it means propagating retention, and indoctrinating various talents into an organizational culture of innovation and production efficiency. It is so absurd that as of date, Nigeria cannot account for millions of her talents scattered all over the world and building other nations. Leading and organizing go hand-in-hand, and for any transformation process to effectively occur in this region, Nigeria must unify these talents and draw necessary resources for a collective transformation forum.

Overhauling Nigerian culture of governance is one thing, but constructing a transformation strategy without destructive consequences requires some OD competence. A transformation process by agents unfamiliar with the OD language would be like engaging carpenters for auto repairs.

(1) **Gallos, J.V. (2006, 2007).** *Organization development.* An Francisco, CA; Jossey-Bass.

III

PORTRAITS OF TYRANNY

8

Inglorious Dictators: The Assault of the AK-47 Confraternity

■ The culture of Nigerian governance thus became a career for trigger-loving army numbskulls, with no formal leadership training. As a matter of record, it is disappointing to note that none of the Military leaders that ruled Nigeria after the civil war in 1970 had a college degree, or a corresponding training to suite that official capacity.

One major question that challenges my intellect and may have equally puzzled many observers and thinkers in social science is how a verified rich nation, potential goldmine *per say*, could be bastardized beyond recognition by brainless despots into political insecurity, economic vagueness, uncontrolled criminality, and communal wretchedness. Nigeria's economic prosperity or potential was never in doubt, for even a blind man could see that clearly.

■ **Nigerian Army:** View of Jaji Military Cantonment, about 30 kilometers (19 miles) north of the city of Kaduna.
Observers and thinkers in social science are still puzzled on how a verified rich nation, potential goldmine per say, could be bastardized beyond recognition, by brainless army dictators into political insecurity, economic vagueness, uncontrolled criminality, and communal wretchedness.

Mohammed Salisu of Lancaster University Management School expounded on this issue. Salisu[1] in a paper about Nigeria wrote, "With a per capita income of around $1100 during the late 1970s Nigeria was regarded as the fastest growing country in sub-Saharan Africa, thanks to the oil windfall. Since then Nigeria has been rarely off the world press, but mostly due to notoriety rather than fame." Consequently, International Monetary Fund (IMF) in its Poverty Reduction Strategy Paper on Nigeria echoed a similar sentiment, and rendered this analysis;

> "Although revenues from crude oil have been increasing over the past decades, our people have been falling deeper into poverty. In 1980 an estimated 27 percent of Nigerians lived in poverty. By 1990, 70 percent of the population had income of less than $1 a day—and the figure has risen since then. Poverty levels vary across the country, with the highest proportion of poor people in the northwest and the lowest in the southeast."

IMF's paper citing poverty and inequality contended that more than two-thirds of the Nigerian people are poor, despite living in a country with vast potential wealth. Hence, multiple studies and researches published about these sweltering issues redundantly emphasized and reemphasized a culture of corruption and maladministration, whereas major faces behind the catastrophe were left out of deliberation.

It is a fact that after the civil war, Nigeria had the chance to bounce back to a projected glory, but a repeated nature of military coups, upon military coups punctuated any progress, and created the greatest damage yet in the economic history of this country. The coup tradition, after the civil war in 1970 started

(1) **Salisu, M.** (2000) Corruption in Nigeria . Lancaster University.

■ Intellectually Bankrupt: **Gowon,** it may be recalled, went to school and in fact attained his first college degree after ruling Nigeria from 1966-75

with General Murtala Muhammed whose overthrow of a post war regime led by General Yakubu Gowon in 1975 opened up another traditional phase of leadership by coups and governance by punitive decrees. It was an era of leadership by AK-47 – or leadership under the influence of illiteracy, alcohol, and assault rifles. AK-47 officially known as Avtomat Kalashnikova is a Russian-made assault rifle very synonymous with the military cabals that held on to power till 1993 – a hellish 18-year period.

Even before his removal, Gowon remained a timid unkempt soldier whose knowledge is limited to operating minor assault rifles. The then inaudible, haggardly-looking man strived to unite the country and soften the mistrust and anger created by the civil war. Nonetheless, his avowals of "No Victor-No Vanquished" philosophy brought some courage and instilled some hope for a united populace.

But it might be relevant to assess what Gowon had in his brains as the leader of Africa's most populous country. He had no theoretical vision, no blue print for the revitalization of a country devastated by a three-year war. In a thorough assessment, as far as strategic economic management of his leadership command is concerned, it was a pitiful write-off. Hence, the biggest economic blunder ever committed in Nigeria's history occurred in 1974 during Gowon's tenure. It was in 1974 when Nigeria experienced the greatest oil boom. Gowon, academically bankrupt, and who could not read his left from right without a how-to-do-it manual ended up bastardizing any prudent foundation that could have helped his successors. This did not come as a surprise. Gowon, it may be recalled, went to school and in fact attained his first college degree after ruling Nigeria from 1966-75, prompting the disparaging effects of leadership before basic training.

Brigadier (later General) Muhammad established himself as a Nigerian leader through a coup, July 29, 1975, that ousted General Gowon while the latter was at an Organization of African Unity (OAU) summit in Kampala, Uganda. Brigadiers Obasanjo (later Lt. General) and Danjuma (later Lt. General) were appointed as Chief of Staff, Supreme Headquarters and Chief of Army Staff, respectively. Leadership of this country at the time became a turn-by-turn affair with core governmental positions reserved for even officers still in training.

The culture of Nigerian governance thus became a career for trigger-loving army numbskulls, with no formal leadership training. As a matter of record, it is disappointing to note that none of the Military leaders that ruled Nigeria after the civil war in 1970 had a college degree, or a corresponding training to suite their official capacities. Of course, competence matters in leadership. Level of emotional intelligence counts in strategic management; Research[1] suggests that emotional intelligence is responsible for as much as 80% of the "success" in our lives."

Furthermore, intelligence and competence go hand-in-hand. Level of intelligence often propels competence. In the broadest sense, competency refers to an individual's capacity to decide or to perform activities of daily living.[2] Among these, as relate to presidential tasks, are the capacities to work, make executive decisions, and perform assigned responsibilities as required by the constitution. Therefore, leaving a complex multi-tribal and economically challenged nation under some inglorious army officers with underprivileged brainpower was not the best – but it happened in Nigeria.

Mohammad came drunk in coercive power; tormented the nation with punitive decrees, whereas he made core administrative changes to impress potential critics and observers. To break links with Gowon, Mohammad removed top federal and state officials. In what became one of the worst assaults in the civil service, and defilement of civil rights, the mean-looking officer dismissed more than 10,000 public officials and employees without benefits, citing age, health, incompetence, or malpractice. The purge tore down families, and swept through the civil service, judiciary, police and armed forces, diplomatic service, public corporations, and universities.

In furtherance of the bloody tradition of leadership by AK-47, Murtala Mohammed was killed February 13, 1976 - a little less than eight months in office, in an abortive coup led by Lt. Col Buka Suka Dimka. Second in command, Obasanjo took

---

(1) **Freedman, et al.,** Handle With Care: Emotional Intelligence Activity Book
(2) **Denney, R. L., & Wynkoop, T. F.** (2000). Clinical neuropsychology in the criminal forensic setting. *Journal of Head Trauma Rehabilitation.*

over the leadership, inheriting high oil revenues that increased 350 percent between 1973 and 1974. Revenue from the oil boom was drained in wasteful spending and daylight public-fund embezzlement; a situation that translated to a minor recession in 1978-79.

Obasanjo, equally corrupt to the core, actually respected an anticipated return to democratic rule, handing over power to Alhaji Shehu Shagari through an election process. This chance for a civil rule lasted for just a four-year term before another coup struck in December 31, 1983; thus Nigeria's dream for a second republic was barbarically punctuated by General Muhammadu Buhari's armed crew. President Shehu Shagari's government was ejected from power in a palace coup, ending Nigeria's Second Republic. Buhari became Head of State, and Chairman of the Supreme Military Council of Nigeria. (See Chapter 9).

Major shocker in Buhari's gatecrash into power took a turn for the worst, and displayed the height of tyranny and oppression. In fact, the punitive measures that clouded this leadership tormented citizens, and chastised families with reckless abandon. I witnessed, under Buhari, and his second-in-command, General Tunde Idiagbon, civil servants denied pay-checks for being unable to recite the national anthem; I witnessed low-level business owners horse-whipped in the public for not hoisting national flags in their business locations. That was Buhari's idea of being patriotic: flying the Nigerian flag even while asleep, or singing the anthem at a gun-point. The duo, Buhari/Idiagbon launched what was tagged "War Against Indiscipline," (WAI) vowing to cleanse the country from a culture of treachery.

Buhari's approach to leadership took the form of the Taliban, inflicting the country with the most stringent rules through tyrannical decrees.

■ Executive brainlessness: **General Abacha** was one of those army barrack numbskulls who could barely spell their country's name in ink.

Buhari didn't last for too long, before his turn ran out. General Ibrahim Badamasi Babangida (IBB) who was Buhari's Chief of Army Staff and a member of the Supreme Military Council (SMC) gate-crashed into power in August 1985 in a bloodless military coup, promising to bring to an end the prevailing human rights abuses. IBB monopolized power and controlled it like a personal project till his departure in August 27, 1993. Initially, he came in smiling at the cameras, and in a phony attempt to distinguish himself from other dictators, he touted a human side of his military dexterity. He softened some harsh decrees constituted by his predecessors, especially the death penalty for heinous offenses, just to woo support and love from the suffering masses. That was IBB, a purported devil's reincarnate who apparently made more victims that Uganda's Idi Amin, and Apollo Milton Obote put together, but subdues every evidence to physically link him to his deeds. (See Chapter 10). He was miraculously forced out of office by a worldwide combined pressure.

Next Khaki man on line, who was IBB's second-in-command, General Sani Abacha seized up power. Abacha quietly, but strategically took over power from the interim government of Chief Ernest Shonekan, installed by IBB. IBB's annulment of a controversial 12 June 1993, it may be recalled caused an enormous widespread tumult that led to his resignation. Abacha who took over power was one of those army barrack numbskulls who could barely spell their country's name in ink. His regime only witnessed a continuation of IBB duplicitous and bloody tenure. Abacha, it may be recalled, was tied to human rights violations and allegations of corruption.

Abacha went on rampage with the opposition, reinforcing his killer-squad with more responsibilities. We may also recall that this dictator authorized the hanging of an Ogoni activist Ken

Saro-Wiwa who bitterly opposed the exploitation of Nigerian resources by the multinational petroleum company, Royal Dutch Shell Group. The politician and philanthropist, believed to have won the Election annulled by IBB, Alhaji Mushood Abiola, and former dictator, Olusegun Obasanjo were jailed for treason, and Nobel Prize winner, Wole Soyinka charged in absentia with the same offense. Besides his hands which were smeared with the blood of the opposition, Abacha ran down Nigeria's treasury through fraudulent money transfers and enrichment of his cronies. To make it worse, an estimated $1.4 billion in cash was reportedly stolen through fictitious transfers alone.

Abacha remained a desperate despot, surrounded himself with approximately 3,000 deadly armed men; defied every opposition and sanctions, and ignored a consistent call by major countries to step down. There was however, one major call Abacha could not curtail – death. Abacha died in June 1998 in the presidential villa in Abuja. His death created another shameful moment to the country's image.Whereas Nigerian military rulers and successors cited the cause of his death as a sudden heart attack, evidence revealed a shocker. According to the report, Abacha was in the company of six teenage Indian prostitutes imported from Dubai, purported to have flavored his drink with poison. Another report claimed he actually died after an overdose of Viagra, having sex with the same prostitutes.

Maj. Gen. Abdulsalami Abubakar, Nigeria's defense chief of staff who had never before held public office was sworn in as the country's head of state. Abubakar's swift announcement of a transition to democracy signaled the end of this military era; so far an end to the invasion of some inglorious juntas into Nigeria's economic, social and political system.

9

Buhari: An Oil Portrait of Despotism

■ Call to duty? A calling perpetrated by a society of redundant military officers inspired by overdose of alcohol, Cannabis, and AK-47 riffles. But the major issue is how a local army without any leadership aptitude besides commanding platoons, barracks, and cantonments, could preside over a complex econo-political entity that is.

"I have sworn upon the altar of God, eternal hostility against every form of tyranny over the mind of man" **(Thomas Jefferson).**

The most dangerous bee is that which lands on your groin. Punch it, you smash your manhood; leave it, and you are stung to death. For Nigeria, General Muhammadu Buhari (rtd) is that killer-bee on the balls, wheezing for a destructive sting. He has been involved—one way or the other—in every Nigerian military rule since the civil war; participated in coups; and

■ For Nigeria, **General Muhammadu Buhari (rtd)** (pictured) is that killer-bee on the balls, wheezing for a destructive sting.

as a retired junta member, ran three presidential races without a scrap of success. In 2003 he lost the presidential election to incumbent Olusegun Obasanjo and refused to concede; in 2007 he failed woefully in the presidential polls against the late president Yar'Adua, and unsuccessfully took his protest to court to no avail; and in 2011, he lost the presidential election again to Goodluck Ebele Jonathan and headed to the court houses for another failed miracle.

Nigerians who were fifty years in 2012 were barely one year when Muhammadu Buhari joined the army. This he did in 1962. He has since remained one of those former students of the Nigerian Defense Academy (NDA), who used their training to wrestle legitimate power out of the system, rather than defend the country's security needs. Born December 17, 1942, in the town of Daura in the former Katsina province of the then Northern Nigeria, he attended elementary school in Daura and Mai'adua from 1948 – 1952; Katsina middle School in 1953; Katsina Provincial Secondary School 1956 – 1961 - then proceeded to the Nigerian Military Training School, Kaduna in 1963.

Buhari, additionally attended a series of military-based trainings, and held positions at various capacities, and took active part in Nigeria's civil war where millions of kids perished.The repulsive thing about Buhari's career, which centered on soldiering, is how these skills were utilized into political play to create a culture that held Nigeria's leadership development evolution to ransom with nonsensical coup-de'tats. Besides his civil war oppressive records, Buhari's assault of Nigeria's political progress was capped by destroying the country's first presidential system – setting the stage for other tyrannical dictators that came after him. How exactly did Buhari do that?

In Nigeria, December 31 is cherished as the last day of the year; new year's eve, that is; when, out of cheerfulness, the sounds of Chinese crackers, bamboo bangers, red banger fireworks, or flash bangers interrupt the nights tranquility, but dies down way after midnight to usher in the new year. But the first day of New Year after December 31, 1983 wasn't quite like others, because the preceding New Year didn't come as joyous as the previous years. The radio, and television programs that often feature song-praises, and New Year messages, and well-wishes, and songs requests were interrupted by this non-stop marshal music that went for hours without any announcements. From Beethoven's *"Wellington's Victory,"* Prokofiev's *"War Sonatas"* or *"Battle on the Ice,"* to Shostakovich's *Symphony No.7, "* there was no doubt that the entire country, Africa's most populous, was under siege.

At this time, those familiar with Nigeria's system knew that something was happening to the country's leadership. Of course, it must be a coup, for confirmation and other details were a matter of time. At some point, the announcement finally came. It was exactly January 1, 1984 - Major-General Buhari has taken over the legitimate government headed by Alhaji Shegu Shagari .

His speech in part:

> "In pursuance of the primary objective of saving our great nation from total collapse, I, Major-General Muhammadu Buhari of the Nigerian army have, after due consultation amongst the services of the armed forces, been formally invested with the authority of the Head of the Federal Military Government and the Commander-in-Chief of the armed forces of the Federal Republic of Nigeria. It is with humility and a deep sense

of responsibility that I accept this challenge and call to national duty." (See full text on page 119).

Which duty? A calling perpetrated by a society of redundant military officers inspired by overdose of alcohol, cannabis, and AK-47 riffles, and headed by a desperate chump behind the radio announcement proclaiming himself the Commander-in-Chief of the armed forces of the Federal Republic of Nigeria. But the major issue is how a local army without any leadership aptitude besides commanding platoons, barracks, and cantonments, could preside over a complex econo-political entity that is.

Buhari's gate-crashing into a leadership suite bigger than his brainpower may not be the only travesty; his values were another destructive trait. He was one of those conservative Muslim fanatics with the heart of Hamas, a propensity equal to those of Al Qaeda, and the vision of Taliban; one of those who would question God for creating any being other than a Muslim; or even challenge Him for creating women.

You can look at his face and tell his destructive sexist characteristics; a cerebrum of masculinity that impels a dominating attitude over women in such that subjugates their self-confidence, intimidate them, humiliate them in public by devaluing their opinion, and render them less powerful than any male. No wonder, his cabinet, announced shortly after his coup has no single woman. To him, gender consideration is a western movie, and women should be perpetually confined to the purdah. Here is a leader who never mentioned his wives or children at any public forum, or in his official biographic information; a clear confirmation of his repressive quality.

So, how could such destructive ideologies influence the demeanor of a dictator? Buhari came at a time when the general public were still dealing with the negative consequences of a recent civil war, and another horror springing from ravages of an experimental four-year executive system presided by Alhaji Shagari.

Anybody can be a leader, but definitely, not anybody can lead a complex economy of a country riddled with hard-hitting socio-political issues. Also, it is a fact that leadership skills could be acquired but always, situations may differ. Leadership, according to Burns[1] is a two-part process, where followers could transform leaders by sheer interaction. Burns had argued that leaders may increase the confidence of followers as well as inspire their expectations of success. So how could these concepts correspond the intellectual bearing of the dictator?

There are no suggestions or studies that leadership is a reserve of a certain class, or tribe, or even made for some specific ranks of the army. The notion is simple, that anybody can be a leader, but not every leader can successfully deliver. Whereas the Trait Era[2] of late 1800s to Mid-1940s believed that leaders are born rather than made, "More than 40 years of study provided little or no evidence to justify that assertion – an indication that anybody (entrepreneur or otherwise) could be a great leader if the proper mechanisms are applied.

Confirmed Navahandi,[3] we all can learn to become better leaders; great leaders spend time to communicate, effectively manage conflicts, empower, develop, and motivate constituents, and it takes a humble person to meet these demands.

---

(1) Burns, J. A. (1995). Transactional and Transformational Leadership. In J.T. Wren (ed.), The leader's companion: Insights on leadership through the ages. New York: The Free Press.
(2-3) Navahandi Afsaneh (2006). the Art and Science of Leadership, Fourth Edition, Published by Prentice Hall.

The fundamental concepts that determine good leadership may depend on a number of different approaches, but brutality is not one of them. Individually, simulations are based on a combination of beliefs, values and preferences. Furthermore, researchers provided some links associating personality and behavior to performance. Navahandi asserts that personality is a stable set of physical and psychological characteristics that makes each person unique[1]. Again, Navahandi, advised that "Three major individual different characteristics can affect leadership style: personality, values, and skills."[2]

On the contrary, Buhari's personality in his retributive rule was a nightmare. He projected himself like a Roman god, and ruled like the Taliban. Wole Soyinka, the Nigerian-born Nobel Laureate wrote of Buhari's iron heart, and the animalistic instinct that drove his leadership thus:

> "Prominent against these charges was an act that amounted to nothing less than judicial murder, the execution of a citizen under a retroactive decree. Does Decree 20 ring a bell? If not, then, perhaps the names of three youths – Lawal Ojuolape (30), Bernard Ogedengbe (29) and Bartholomew Owoh (26) do. To put it quite plainly, one of those three Ogedengbe – was executed for a crime that did not carry a capital forfeit at the time it was committed. This was an unconscionable crime, carried out in defiance of the pleas and protests of nearly every sector of the Nigerian and international community religious, civil rights, political, trade unions etc. Buhari and his sidekick and his partner-in-crime, Tunde Idiagbon persisted in this inhuman act for one

(1-2) **Navahandi Afsaneh** (2006, p. 63)

reason and one reason only: to place Nigerians on notice that they were now under an iron, inflexible rule, under governance by fear."

Soyinka knew where he was headed to with his analysis. Buhari, and second-in-command, Tunde Idiagbon designated as the Chief of General Staff had justified the power seizure with the usual excuses of despondently corrupt civilian rulership.

To sway attention from the questionability of their objectives, his administration consequently initiated a public campaign against indiscipline branded as "War Against Indiscipline" (WAI); encompassing another action to enforce patriotism among citizens. Overnight, Nigeria was transformed into torture courtyard, with Taliban laws systematically imposed to her diverse populace. Timeline of Buhari's WAI were as follows;

a. Queuing (March 20, 1984)

b. Work Ethics (May 1, 1984)

c. Nationalism and Patriotism (August 21, 1984)

d. Anti-Corruption and Economic Sabotage (May 14, 1985)

e. Environmental Sanitation (July 29, 1985).

In a more scholarly analysis, the above five-point agenda reflects practicable demands in ethical philosophies, and in fact, represents positive transformational tools in organizational change. Nonetheless, the execution must necessitate a well-thought-out competence to define the implementation effectiveness. Nigeria is a multi-culture environment where complexities of tribes and tongues could easily derail any organizational design approach. Thus ethics management across such cultures be complicated; but that is one of the major demands of management philosophy. No wonder, Jones,[1] examined how ethical behavior could be promoted so that, at the very least, organizational members are able to resist any temptation to engage in illegal acts that promote personal or organizational interests at the expense of the members of the society.

Beneath the notion that leaders can design an organizational structure that reduces the incentives for people who behave unethically, Jones, argued that the creation of authority relationships and rules that promote ethical behavior and punish unethical acts, for example, encourages members to behave in a socially responsible way. [2] Consequently, Bateman – Snell argued that maintaining consistent ethical behavior by subordinates is an ongoing challenge, not a one-night stand.

Culture and ethics are knotted as effective management philosophies but could be complicated in general application. Leaders therefore, must be careful about the technicalities of operating under cultural vision, and adherence to ethical vision. For instance, Buhari's Islamic doctrine undermines any motivational approach to ethics, and encourages ethical enforcement through corporal punishment and severe torture.

Ethics, according to Jones defines appropriate and inappropriate behaviors, and sets the standards on how individuals should behave to avoid doing harm to others.[3] Application, however could be complicated. According to Jones, "The essential problem in dealing with ethical issues, and thus solving moral dilemmas, is that no absolute or indisputable rules or principles can be developed to decide if an action is ethical or unethical,"[1] yet Buhari and his men chose to delve into such

1, 2, 3) **Jones, G.R.** (2010). Organizational theory, design, and change (6th Ed.)
(2) **Bateman, T. S., & Snell, S. A.** (2007, p. 156). Management: Leading and collaborating in a competitive world (7th ed.).

concepts tyrannically.

It was awful, as fierce-looking soldiers armed to their teeth were ordered to torture small businesses unable to hoist Nigerian flags in their facilities. Senior citizens were humiliatingly asked to recite the national pledge or sing the national anthems before they could receive their pensions; and same laws applied to some federal employees who had to sing to receive paychecks. Soldiers used horse whips at public places to torture people for minor public behaviors. For instance, I witnessed how a pregnant woman was dragged in the back of an antiquated army Land Rover jeep for helplessly easing herself beside a grassy road path; a cab driver dragged out of his car, made to lie face down on a dusty road for jumping the queue; an aged woman being manhandled by soldiers who accused her for replying them with too much grammar, and so on.

Buhari may be right in his expectation of a disciplined society. Good character is good and is expected in any civil society; for even late Idi Amin,[2] one of Africa's worst dictators, understood that philosophy. From a scholarly perspective, however, Premeaux [3] unveiled technicalities of the ethical system by advocating effective approaches in managing moral philosophy. Bateman & Snell [4] describe moral philosophy as rules, and values used in making decisions on what is right or wrong.

But as Premeaux noted, applying the moral tradition in any

(1) **Jones, G.R.** (2010, p. 44). Organizational theory, design, and change (6th Ed.)
(2) **Idi Amin Dada** (1920 –2003); third President of Uganda (1971 to 1979) whose rule was characterized by human rights abuse, political repression, ethnic persecution, extrajudicial killings, nepotism, corruption, and gross economic mismanagement *(Wikipedia, the free encyclopedia)*.
(3) **Premeaux, S.** (2009). The link between management behavior and ethical philosophy in the wake of the Enron convictions.
(4) **Bateman, T. S., & Snell, S. A.** (2007). Management: Leading and collaborating in a competitive world (7th ed.).

organization requires some systematic approach devoid of cruelty. With citizens still dealing with austerity measures implemented by the previous administration to address a dwindling economy, curbing bribery and corruption requires a blue print that would address other economic and socio political issues.

Strategy may not just be enough, but also, it would require some humility and charisma to deal with a domain immersed by a lack of basic amenities; where frustrations developed out of starvation and unemployment ignite corruption rate.

Ousted President Shagari was a humble man, but totally lacked any organizational development strategies to save his country from economic and socio-political woes. But he was legitimately elected and ought to have been removed through a constitutionally allowed process – definitely not through a senseless coup by overzealous army dissidents.

Consequently, Buhari's tyrannical conduct and the Nigerian situation raise another issue about leadership and ability traits. Nigeria needed a leader with mental ability; she needed a humble leader – charismatic by nature or design, with the heart of Mother Theresa, wisdom of Bill Clinton, and the sureness of Barack Obama. A humble leader is charismatic because he overlooks ego, acknowledges contributions of others, respects subordinates, and ignores public exaltation. The Charismatic Leadership is based on personality and charm, rather than any form of external power or authority. Nadler listed three major behaviors that characterize a charismatic leader, as envisioning, energizing, and enabling. [1]

Nonetheless, Buhari brought to the table, his obsessive Is-

---

(1) Bateman, T. S., & Snell, S. A. (2007). Management: Leading and collaborating in a competitive world (7th ed.).

lamic ideology; a quest to forceful persuasion of subjects into impracticable Islamic laws under the disguise of fighting corruption. To further this mission, Buhari relied heavily on decrees and special tribunals to regulate communal life and chastise offenders. For instance, he had promulgated a decree imposing life imprisonment on anyone found guilty of corruption. In yet another display of his tyrannical brainless decision-making scheme, Buhari initiated four tribunals, chaired by appointed army officers, but comprising three senior officers and a judge, to try hundreds of allegedly corrupt politicians detained under his command. Now, what would a learned high court judge be doing with such a panel of ignorant army officers?

As of July 1984, Buhari had promulgated as much as twenty-two decrees, radiating controversies and international condemnation. Two major decrees underscored Buhari's totalitarian cleverness; Decree Number 4 prohibited any journalist from reporting information considered embarrassing to any government official, while Decree Number 2 empowered the chief of Staff to detain anyone considered a security risk for up to six months without trial. The judiciary was subjugated by special military tribunals whereas the state security agency, the National Security Organization, was accorded greater powers.

Buhari's assault of his nation did not stand a test of the tide. In a leadership suit of dictators where trust, respect, and transparency lacked, security is often dicey. Exactly on August 27, 1985, Buhari was equally ousted in a coup led by another bloodthirsty despot, General Ibrahim Babangida. Babangida had rallied other members of the ruling Supreme Military Council (SMC) critical of Buhari to execute a smooth palace coup.

But Nigeria should be worried that Buhari, since his removal as a dictator, has not given up in his quest for the topmost position. Disappointed that he was not given a chance to totally transform Nigeria's governmental system into a Taliban-modeled structure, this man had declared a desperate return to accomplish his mission, but things keep getting ugly. For instance, in 2003, he lost the presidential election to a former army colleague, Olusegun Obasanjo. In 2007, he lost another presidential election to late Yar'Adua; and finally, in 2011, he lost the presidential election to current president, Goodluck Jonathan. (Also, see page 107, para. 1).

The bad signs of Buhari, and Nigeria's sociopolitical progress, therefore is his desperate aspiration to return to a presidential seat he forcefully occupied and defiled years ago. Hence, if the population of current Nigerian generation ever allows another travesty of their political progress and economic prosperity, they should blame themselves for a self-destructive attitude.

Nigeria actually needs some kind of leadership that makes sense; effective and consistent with every transformational outline. Effective leadership prioritizes a creation of shared vision to cushion a projected future for constituents. Instilling such vision creates economic stability, a sense of direction, and operational efficiency. Tichy and Devanna[1] added that "The vision is the ideal to strive for. It releases the energy needed to motivate the organization to action. It provides an overarching framework to guide day-to-day decisions and priorities and provides the parameters for planful opportunism."

Realizing a vision may be practically impossible without implanting trust and hope into the masses. The success of trans-

---

(1)Tichy N. M., and Devanna M. A. (1990, p. 62) the Transformational Leader: The Key to Global Competitiveness

formational and charismatic leadership is definitely not through forceful persuasion, but lies in the ability to charm subordinates with some fundamental behavioral traits. For instance, Nadler as it was stated earlier (page 115) ascribed this to envisioning, energizing, and enabling.[1]

Organizational leadership entails charming subordinates through a set of competencies to attain projected success and greatness. Navahandi explained how personality as a stable set of physical and psychological characteristics make each person unique. Success, however, may be dependent to organizational environment. For instance, Contingency Model as explained by Navahandi, requires personality, style, or behavior of effective leaders but depends on the demands of the situation in which leaders find themselves. Buhari's situation is indisputably a wedge-shaped peg in a square hole.

(1) **Nadler, David A. and Tushman Michael L.** (1995, p. 109). Beyond the Charismatic Leader: Leadership and Organizational Change. In J.T. Wren (ed.).

Inaugural Speech of Major-General Muhammadu Buhari.

■ January 1, 1984.

———————◆———————

In pursuance of the primary objective of saving our great nation from total collapse, I, Major-General Muhammadu Buhari of the Nigerian army have, after due consultation amongst the services of the armed forces, been formally invested with the authority of the Head of the Federal Military Government and the Commander-in-Chief of the armed forces of the Federal Republic of Nigeria. It is with humility and a deep sense of responsibility that I accept this challenge and call to national duty.

As you must have heard in the previous

announcement, the constitution of the Federal Republic of Nigeria (1979) has been suspended, except those sections of it which are exempted in the constitution.The change became necessary in order to put an end to the serious economic predicament and the crisis of confidence now afflicting our nation. Consequently, the Nigerian armed forces have constituted themselves into a Federal Military Government comprising of a Supreme Military Council, a National Council of States, a Federal Executive Council at the centre and State Executive Councils to be presided over by military governors in each of the states of the federation. Members of these councils will be announced soon.The last Federal Military Government drew up a programme with the aim of handing over political power to the civilians in 1979. This programme as you all know, was implemented to the letter. The 1979 constitution was promulgated. However, little did the military realise that the political leadership of the second republic will circumvent most of the checks and balances in the constitution and bring the present state of general insecurity. The premium on political power became so exceedingly high that political contestants regarded victory at elections as a matter of life and death struggle and were determined to capture or retain power by all means.

It is true that there is a worldwide economic recession. However, in the case of Nigeria, its impact was aggravated by mismanagement. We believe the appropriate government agencies have good advice but the leadership disregarded their advice. The situation could have been avoided if the legislators were alive to their constitutional responsibilities; Instead, the legislators were preoccupied with determining their salary scales, fringe benefit and unnecessary foreign travels, et al, which took no account of the state of the economy and the welfare of the people they represented. As a result of our inability to cultivate financial discipline and prudent management of the economy, we have come to depend largely on internal and external borrowing to execute government projects with attendant domestic pressure and soaring external debts, thus aggravating the propensity of the outgoing civilian administration to mismanage our financial resources. Nigeria was already condemned perpetually with the twin problem of heavy budget deficits and weak balance of payments position, with the prospect of building a virile and viable economy.

The last general election was anything

but free and fair. The only political parties that could complain of election rigging are those parties that lacked the resources to rig. There is ample evidence that rigging and thuggery were relative to the resources available to the parties. This conclusively proved to us that the parties have not developed confidence in the presidential system of government on which the nation invested so much material and human resources.While corruption and indiscipline have been associated with our state of under-development, these two evils in our body politic have attained unprecedented height in the past few years. The corrupt, inept and insensitive leadership in the last four years has been the source of immorality and impropriety in our society. Since what happens in any society is largely a reflection of the leadership of that society, we deplore corruption in all its facets. This government will not tolerate kick-backs, inflation of contracts and over-invoicing of imports etc. Nor will it condone forgery, fraud, embezzlement, misuse and abuse of office and illegal dealings in foreign exchange and smuggling.

Arson has been used to cover up fraudulent acts in public institutions. I am referring to the fire incidents that gutted the P&T buildings in Lagos, the Anambra State

Broadcasting Corporation, the Republic Building at Marina, the Federal Ministry of Education, the Federal Capital Development Authority Accounts at Abuja and the NET Building. Most of these fire incidents occurred at a time when Nigerians were being apprehensive of the frequency of fraud scandals and the government incapacity to deal with them. Corruption has become so pervasive and intractable that a whole ministry has been created to stem it. Fellow Nigerians, this indeed is the moment of truth. My colleagues and I – the Supreme Military Council, must be frank enough to acknowledge the fact that at the moment, an accurate picture of the financial position is yet to be determined. We have no doubt that the situation is bad enough. In spite of all this, every effort will be made to ensure that the difficult and degrading conditions under which we are living are eliminated. Let no one however be deceived that workers who have not received their salaries in the past eight or so months will receive such salaries within today or tomorrow or that hospitals which have been without drugs for months will be provided with enough immediately. We are determined that with the help of God we shall do our best to settle genuine payments to which government is committed, including backlog of workers' salaries after scrutiny. We are confident and we assure you that even in the face of the global recession, and the seemingly gloomy financial future, given prudent management of Nigeria's existing financial resources and our determination to substantially reduce and eventually nail down rises in budgetary deficits and weak balance of payments position.The Federal Military Government will reappraise policies with a view to paying greater attention to the following areas:

• The economy will be given a new impetus and better sense of direction.

• Corrupt officials and their agents will be brought to book.

• In view of the drought that affected most parts of the country, the federal government will, with the available resources, import food stuffs to supplement the shortfalls suffered in the last harvest.

Our foreign policy will both be dynamic and realistic. Africa will of course continue to be the centre piece of our foreign policy. The morale and combat readiness of the armed forces will be given high priority. Officers and men with high personal and professional integrity will have nothing to fear.

The Chief Justice of Nigeria and all other holders of judiciary appointments within the federation can continue in their appointments and the judiciary shall continue to function under existing laws subject to such exceptions as may be decreed from time to time by the Federal Military Government. All holders of appointments in the civil service, the police and the National Security Organisation shall continue to exercise their functions in the normal way subject to changes that may be introduced by the Federal Military Government. All those chairmen and members of statutory corporations, parastatals and other executive departments are hereby relieved of their appointments with immediate effect.

The Federal Military Government will maintain and strengthen existing diplomatic relations with other states and with international organisations and institutions such as the Organisation of African Unity, the United Nations and its organs, Organisation of Petroleum Exporting Countries, ECOWAS and the Commonwealth etc. The Federal Military Government will honour and respect all treaties and obligations entered into by the previous government and we hope that such nations and bodies will reciprocate this gesture by respecting our country's territorial integrity and sovereignty.

Fellow Nigerians, finally, we have dutifully intervened to save this nation from imminent collapse. We therefore expect all Nigerians, including those who participated directly or indirectly in bringing the nation to this present predicament, to cooperate with us. This generation of Nigerians, and indeed future generations, have no country other than Nigeria. We shall remain here and salvage it together.

May God bless us all. Good morning.

10

IBB: Toxic Portrait of a Tyrant

■ He wore a bleached smiling face, gap-tooted, and spoke English with an adulterated Fulani-Kanuri accent, while his seat of sensation remains a million worse than a retarded gutter snipe. His deeds made Nigeria's history an X-rated Halloween horror film, most notably with his brutal murder of journalist, Dele Giwa.

It would be hard to forget one of Nigeria's blackest moments—a period accredited to the mysterious handiworks of former Nigeria's dictator, General Ibrahim Badamosi Babangida (aka IBB) which consisted of vanishing or killing of journalists, and military personnel. Let us consider the horrible "unseen plot" of the Ejigbo, Lagos crash of a Nigerian Air Force C-130 plane where 146, mainly young southern army officers perished in what was ranked among the world's 50 worst air crashes (military and civilian) in international aviation history.

■ **General Ibrahim Badamosi Babangida (aka IBB)** made more victims than Idi Amin and Milton Obote put together but was miraculously forced out of office by a combined worldwide pressure. Surprisingly, wonders never end because IBB as of 2010 was still active, aspiring to warm himself back to the same seat he misused and abused.

Apart from the facts that the "C-130H" has three engines, four main fuel tanks, and two auxiliary tanks located in the wings, this aircraft was strongly build to crash-land on land or sea. There were movements, and secret orders within the IBB Killer-squad suite, therefore the worst was being expected. As I was a journalist who thrived and survived IBB's era in the mid-eighties, such expectations of horrible deeds or other atrocities were common. Most of the times, we were grounded in the grapevine world gathering information and holding discussion forums through whispers to avoid being the next victims.

Before this ill-fated flight made its final trip, there was also reportedly, an alteration of flight schedules to make sure all targeted officers were bound into the killer- C-130 Hercules. We knew IBB had targeted most oppositions in government and media as well as rivals in the military circle, but no one knew it would be a sorry sight of bloody deed. As flight NAA911 finally took off, unusual problems immediately began. First engine failed, forcing the pilot to turn around, heading back to the airport; then the second engine failed, leaving the plane without enough power and lift to negotiate and proceed with the airport return. This was when the pilot decided to land the plane in the Ejigbo Canal. To make it worse, the third engine failed subsequently without warning, forcing the plane to nose-dive into the swamp, with fuselage buried in the mud.

Victims were mainly IBB military-foes and young promising top and mid-level officers; and just a few statistics revealed such a tremendous loss of human talents and innocent lives. Figures, for instance, were;

> Army Lt Colonels (7)
> Army Majors (96)
> Army Sergeants (1)
> Civilian Staff (3)

Air Force (26)

Air Force (17)

The fact later surfaced from other investigative journalists, through government sources, that less than an hour after the crash, IBB denied offers by the British and the United States to assist in rescuing the victims. In fact, the U.S. government informed the IBB administration that they had a ship close by and could immediately access the crash, but this offer was turned down.[1]   Besides a phony investigative process of the actual final moments of this unfortunate flight, the major question remained: "What does IBB know?"

In the late 80's, Nigeria's former junta leader, IBB was both a military leader and a mean-hearted demigod. He made more victims than Idi Amin and Milton Obote put together but was miraculously forced out of office by a combined worldwide pressure. Surprisingly, wonders never end because IBB as of 2010 was still active, aspiring to warm himself back to the same seat he misgoverned and abused.

I understand it fully, that in the jungle anything is possible, and so is continental Africa where clean-cut democracy suffers mutilation. I have mentioned it already, many times, that in a country like Nigeria, where free and fair election hardly existed since its independence in 1960, good leadership has remained elusive as retired but corrupt army generals held tight to economic and political powers, and took turns in some kind of public money looting known in this region as "sharing of the national cake."

---

(1) **Military regimes** in Nigeria operated in strict secrecy; most incriminating records of their atrocities were either concealed or confiscated. Eyewitness accounts of victims, leaks from frustrated former employees or agents, however, made it to the media.

IBB is one of such notorious leaders whose damage to his country years back remains a permanent tattoo, but who still flourishes in richness and shockingly, still nurtures insatiable thirst for power. His ascendance to office in 1985 was a chance. He was an erratic Chief of Army Staff who was to be removed by his bosses for security reasons. Buhari told the *Sun News* that he had tabled proposal for the retirement of one Mr. Gusau, the Director of Military Intelligence and a close ally of IBB, and it became clear that IBB could be the next target. This move provoked IBB who organized his loyalists and forced the Buhari regime out.

Another source close to *International Guardian* indicated that IBB was to be removed from office to face a possible interrogation over corruption, but the smart dude quickly took over power while his two bosses, military leader, General Buhari and second-in-command Tunde Idiagbon were on religious pilgrimage.(See IBB's inaugural speech on page 135).

A third version of the story came from Buhari's admirers who believed that he was overthrown by corrupt elements in his government uncomfortable with his strict policies on ethics. IBB and cronies, it was reported, were afraid of being brought to justice as Buhari's war against corruption closed up on them.

But between this time-1985 and 1993, when IBB was forced to step down, he had done more damage than a tsunami, leaving his country Nigeria brain dead, without any social, economic, and political future.

History will forever remember his tenure as the pervert who iniquitously operated with every tool he found necessary, setting up a personal secret service operated from the Middle East, while he dealt with his critics and foes without remorse. He wore a bleached smiling face, gap-tooted, and spoke English with an adulterated Fulani-Kanuri accent, while his seat of sen-

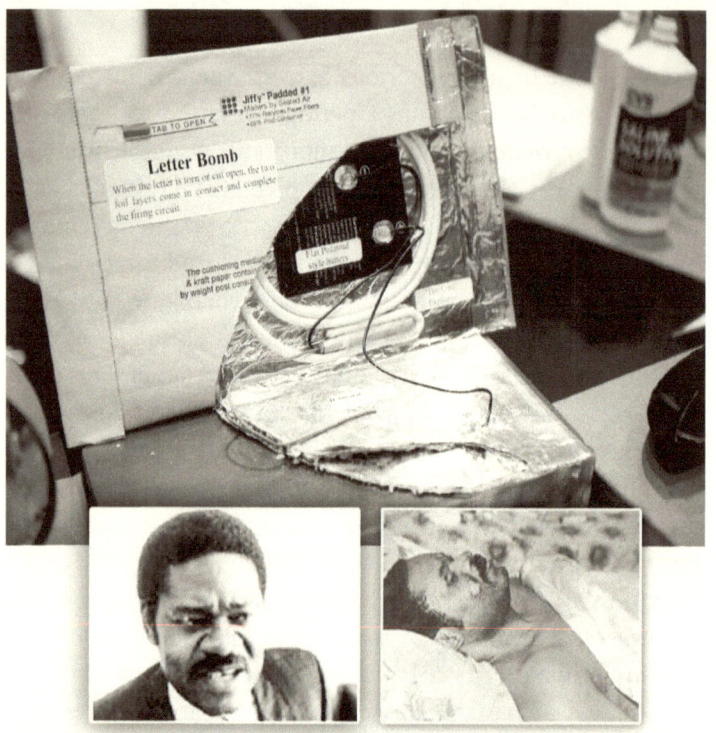

■ **IBB's Legacy:** The letter bomb that delivered the message. **Inset**: Journalist, **Dele Giwa** before and after the blast that permanently hushed his voice.

sation remains detrimentally devilish. His deeds made Nigeria's history an X-rated Halloween horror film, most notably with his brutal murder of journalist, Dele Giwa.

Giwa was killed with a letter bomb for possessing information about one of IBB's drug agents presumed to be dead, but living a secret life in Europe. Using secret agents, stage-managed plane crashes and car wrecks, IBB eliminated his possible rivals and critics, and looted Nigeria's Central Bank with military thugs. Under pressure, IBB later promised to hand over power to a democratically elected leadership, but ended up organizing and supervising the worst transition to civil rule in the history of Nigeria. He set up two political parties by himself, financed their headquarters, and personally handpicked candidates of his choice.

Finally, in June 1993, Nigerians went to the polls to elect Social Democratic Party candidate Moshood Abiola as the new president of the country, with 58 percent of the vote. This victory was short-lived as IBB annulled the election just on the eve of confirmation of results. (See election annulment speech on page 147).

This created unrest and disorganized what analysts described as the only free and fair election since Nigeria's independence, 1960. The below garbage is an excerpt from IBB's infamous June 12 election annulment speech, and this explains the nonsensicality of how these illiterate army officers defiled Nigeria's political progress, and deprived her of any opportunity for advancement for years. IBB's speech read, in part;

> "In the light of our recent experience and, given the mood of the nation, the National Defense and Security Council has imposed additional conditions as a way of widening and deepening the base of electing the president and sanitizing the electoral process. Accordingly, the candidates for the coming election must:
>
> (1) Not be less than 50 years old.
> (2) Have not been convicted of any crime;
> (3) Believe, by act of faith and practice, in the corporate existence of Nigerians;
> (4) Posses records of personal, corporate and business interests which do not conflict with the national interests;

(5) Have been registered members of either of the two political parties for at least one year to this election."

IBB's leadership also witnessed a total lapse in social and economic management. He flip-flopped with the country's economy, setting up a so-called Structural Adjustment Program (SAP) - a subject he totally lacked knowledge of. He intended to devalue the currency, create mass transit and streamline labor force as was advised by his supposedly foreign lenders, so he ended up creating a money-laundering scenario that rendered his country's currency 'Naira' totally valueless, and till date, (2013) Nigeria's fiscal feat has remained in coma. Despite, this chronology of proven misadministration and triviality of transition process, IBB, now singing in a forgive-and forget-tone believed his country was ready to welcome his acclaimed refurbishment. He tried systematically to warm himself back to the system, ran a fake campaign, and made policy comments to woo support.

A probe of IBB's financial misappropriation was supposed to have landed this former general in a place other than politics. If threats of official probity had materialized legally, IBB may have had to spend the rest of his life in an unkempt prison, but in a country where law enforcement and judiciary grasp for survival, political fraudsters hardly go to jail; they head back to the government.

Inaugural Speech of
Major-General Ibrahim Babangida

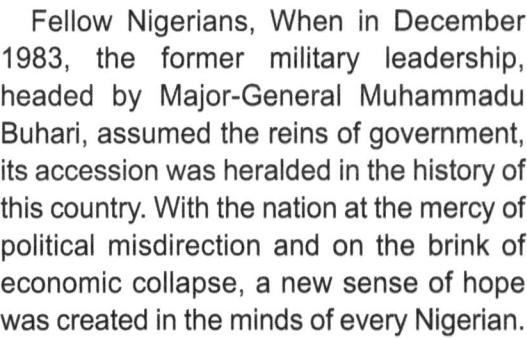

■ August 27 , 1985

Fellow Nigerians, When in December 1983, the former military leadership, headed by Major-General Muhammadu Buhari, assumed the reins of government, its accession was heralded in the history of this country. With the nation at the mercy of political misdirection and on the brink of economic collapse, a new sense of hope was created in the minds of every Nigerian.

Since January 1984, however, we have witnessed a systematic denigration of that hope. It was stated then that mismanagement of political leadership and a general deterioration in the standard of living, which had subjected the common man to intolerable suffering, were the reasons for the intervention.

Nigerians have since then been under a regime that continued with those trends. Events today indicate that most of the reasons which justified the military takeover of government from the civilians still persist.

The initial objectives were betrayed and fundamental changes do not appear on the horizon. Because the present state of uncertainty, suppression and stagnation resulted from the perpetration of a small group, the Nigerian Armed Forces could not as a part of that government be unfairly committed to take responsibility for failure. Our dedication to the cause of ensuring that our nation remains a united entity worthy of respect and capable of functioning as a viable and credible part of the international community dictated the need to arrest the situation.

Let me at this point attempt to make you understand the premise upon which it became necessary to change the leadership. The principles of discussions, consultation and co-operation which should have guided decision-making process of the Supreme Military Council and the Federal Executive Council were disregarded soon after the government settled down in 1984. Where some of us thought it appropriate to give a little more time, anticipating a conducive atmosphere that would develop, in which affairs of state could be attended to with greater sense of responsibility, it became increasingly clear that such expectations could not be fulfilled.

Regrettably, it turned out that Major-General Muhammadu Buhari was too rigid and uncompromising in his attitudes to issues of national significance. Efforts to make him understand that a diverse polity like Nigeria required recognition and appreciation of differences in both cultural and individual perceptions, only served to aggravate these attitudes.

Major-General Tunde Idiagbon was similarly inclined in that respect. As Chief of Staff, Supreme Headquarters, he failed to exhibit the appropriate disposition demanded by his position. He arrogated to himself absolute knowledge of problems and solutions, and acted in accordance with what was convenient to him, using the machinery of government as his tool.

A combination of these characteristics in the two most important persons holding the nation's vital offices became impossible to content with. The situation was made worse by a number of other government functionaries and organisations, chief among which is the Nigerian Security Organisation (NSO). In fact, this body will be overhauled and re-organized.

And so it came to be that the same government which received the tumultuous welcome now became alienated from the people. To prevent a complete erosion of our given mandate therefore, we had to act so that hope may be rebuilt.

Let me now address your attention to the major issues that confront us, so that we may, as one people, chart a future direction for our dear country. We do not pretend to have all the answers to the questions which our present problems have put before our nation. We have come with the strongest determination to create an atmosphere in which positive efforts shall be given the necessary support for lasting solutions.

For matters of the moment which require immediate resolutions, we intend to pursue a determined programme of action. Major issues falling into this category have been identified and decisions taken on what should be done.

Firstly, the issue of political detainees or convicts of special military tribunals. The history of our nation had never recorded the degree of indiscipline and corruption as in the period between October 1979 and

December 1983.

While this government recognises the bitterness created by the irresponsible excesses of the politicians, we consider it unfortunate that methods of such nature as to cause more bitterness were applied to deal with past misdeeds. We must never allow ourselves to lose our sense of natural justice. The innocent cannot suffer the crimes of the guilty. The guilty should be punished only as a lesson for the future. In line with this government's intention to uphold fundamental human rights, the issue of detainees will be looked into with despatch.

As we do not intend to lead a country where individuals are under the fear of expressing themselves, the Public Officers Protection Against False Accusation Decree 4 of 1984 is hereby repealed. And finally, those who have been in detention under this decree are hereby unconditionally released. The responsibility of the media to disseminate information shall be exercised without undue hindrance. In that process, those responsible are expected to be forthright and to have the nation's interest as their primary consideration.

The issue of decrees has generated a lot of controversies. It is the intention of this government to review all other decrees.

The last twenty months have not witnessed any significant changes in the national economy. Contrary to expectations, we have so far been subjected to a steady deterioration in the general standard of living; and intolerable suffering by the ordinary Nigerians have risen higher, scarcity of commodities has increased, hospitals still remain mere consulting clinics, while educational institutions are on the brink of decay. Unemployment has stretched to critical dimensions.

Due to the stalemate, which arose in negotiation with the International Monetary Fund, the former government embarked on a series of counter-trade agreements. Under the counter-trade agreements, Nigerians were forced to buy goods and commodities at higher prices than obtained in the international market. The government intends to review the whole issue of counter-trade.

A lot has been said and heard about our position with the International Monetary Fund. Although we formally applied to the fund in April 1983, no progress has as yet been made in the negotiation and a stalemate has existed for the last two years.

We shall break the deadlock that frustrated the negotiations with a view to evaluating more objectively both the negative and positive implications of reaching a mutual agreement with the Fund. At all times in the course of discussions, our representatives will be guided by the feelings and aspirations of the Nigerian people.

It is the view of this government that austerity without structural adjustment is not the solution to our economic predicament. The present situation whereby 44 per cent of our revenue earning is utilised to service debts is not realistic. To protect the danger this poses to the poor and the needy in our society, steps will be taken to ensure comprehensive strategy of economic reforms.

The crux of our economic problems has been identified to centre around four fundamental issues:

1. A decrease of our domestic production, while our population continues to increase.
2. Dependence on import for both consumer goods and raw materials for our industries.
3. A grossly unequal gap between the rich and the poor.
4. The large role played by the public sector in economic activity with hardly any concrete results to justify such a role.

These are the problems we must confront.

ON FOREIGN POLICY:

Nigeria's foreign policy in the last 20 months has been characterised by inconsistency and incoherence. It has lacked the clarity to make us know where we stood on matters of international concern to enable other countries relate to us with seriousness. Our role as Africa's spokesman has diminished because we have been unable to maintain the respect of African countries.

The ousted military government conducted our external relations by a policy of retaliatory reactions. Nigeria became a country that has reacted to given situations, rather than taking the initiative as it should and always been done. More so, vengeful considerations must not be the basis of our diplomacy. African problems and their solutions should constitute the premise of our foreign policy.

The realisation of the Organisation of African Unity of the Lagos Plan of Action for self-sufficiency and constructive co-operation in Africa shall be our primary pursuit.

The Economic Community of West African States must be reborn with the view to achieving the objective of regional integration. The problems of drought-stricken areas of Africa will be given more attention and sympathy, and our best efforts will be made to assist in their rehabilitation within the limits of our resources. Our membership of the United Nations Organisation will be made more practical and meaningful. The call for a new International Economic Order which lost its momentum in the face of the debt crisis will be made once again.

Nigeria hereby makes a renewed request to the Non-Aligned Movement to regroup and reinvigorate its determination to restructure the global economic system, while we appeal to the industrialized nations to positively consider the debt plight of the developing countries and assist in dealing with the dangers that face us. We shall remain members of the various multilateral institutions and inter-governmental organisations which we belong to and do what must be done to enhance the membership and participation within them.

Fellow Nigerians, this country has had since independence a history mixed with turbulence and fortune. We have witnessed our rise to greatness, followed with a decline to the state of a bewildered nation. Our human potentials have been neglected, our natural resources put to waste. A phenomenon of constant insecurity and overbearing uncertainty has become characteristic of our national existence.

My colleagues and I are determined to

change the course of history. This government is determined to unite this country. We shall not allow anything to obstruct us. We recognise that a government, be it civilian or military, needs the consent of the people to govern if it is to reach its objective. We do not intend to rule by force. At the same time, we should not be expected to submit to unreasonable demands. Fundamental rights and civil liberties will be respected, but their exercise must not degenerate into irrational expression nor border on subversion.

The War Against Indiscipline will continue, but this time, in the minds and conduct of Nigerians, and not by way of symbolism or money-spending campaigns.

This government, on its part, will ensure that the leadership exhibits proper example. Criticisms of actions and decisions taken by us will be given necessary attention and where necessary changes made in accordance with what is expected of us.

Let me reiterate what we said in 1984: This generation of Nigerians and indeed future generations have no other country but Nigeria. We must all stay and salvage it together. This time it shall be pursued with deeper commitment and genuine sincerity.

There is a lot of work to be done by every single Nigerian. Let us all dedicate ourselves to the cause of building a strong, united and viable nation for the sake of our own lives and the benefits of posterity.

Finally, I wish to commend the members of the Armed Forces and the Nigeria Police for their mature conduct during the change.

I thank you all for your co-operation and understanding.

God bless Nigeria.

Speech of General Ibrahim Babangida Invalidating the June 12, 1993 Election

■ June 26, 1993

Fellow Nigerians,

I address you today with a deep sense of world history and particularly of the history of our great country. In the aftermath of the recently annulled Presidential Election, I feel, as I believe you yourself feel, a profound sense of disappointment at the outcome of our last efforts at laying the foundation of a viable democratic system of government in Nigeria .

I therefore wish, on behalf of myself and members of the National Defence and Security Council and indeed of my entire ad-

ministration, to feel with my fellow countrymen and women for the cancellation of the
election. It was a rather disappointing experience in the course of carrying through
the last election of the transition to civil rule
programme.

Nigeria has come a long way since this
administration assumed power and leadership about eight years ago. In the attempt
to grapple with the critical and monumental
problems and challenges of National existence and social progress, this administration inaugurated and pursued sound and
justifiable policies and programmes of reform.

These policies and programmes have
touched virtually all aspects of our national
life – the economy, political process, social
structures, external relations, bureaucracy
and even the family system. I believe
strongly that in understanding, conception,
formulation and articulation, these policies
and programmes are not only sound but
also comparatively unassailable. I believe
too that history, with the passage of time,
would certainly score the administration
high in its governance of our country.

Let me also express my deep conviction
that the core strategy and structures of our
reform policies and programmes, as enunciated in 1986/87 would, for a very long

time, remain relevant and durable in the course of changing our country positively. I believe that at the exit of the Administration from power, we would leave behind for prosperity, a country with an economy, the structures of which have been turned around for good. The average Nigerian person has come to reconcile himself with the fact that his or her social progress remain essentially in his or her hands in collaboration with other fellow Nigerians and not merely relying on what government alone could provide for him or her. The days are gone for good, when men and women trooped to government establishments for employment and for benevolence.

This administration has built the foundation that would take Nigerians away from their previous colonially-induced motivations and the encumbrances of colonialism. We have laid the foundation for self-reliant economic development and social justice. We have established a new basis in our country in which economic liberalization would continue to flourish alongside democratic forces and deregulated power structure. In all these, the average Nigerian person has more than ever before this administration imbibed and assimilated the values of hard work, resilience and self-confidence.

It is true that in the course of implementing our reform policies and programmes and especially because of the visionary zeal with which we approached the assignment and responded to incidental pressures of governance, we engendered a number of social forces in the country.

This is so because we sought to challenge and transform extant social forces which had in the past impeded growth and development of our country. We also sought to deal with the new forces to which our programmes of action gave rise. Thus in dealing with the dynamics of both the old and new social forces, we ran into certain difficulties.

In particular, during the course of handling the interlocking relationships between the old and new political forces and institutions, some problems had arisen leading us into a number of difficulties and thereby necessitating our having to tamper with the rules and regulations laid down in the political programme. As a result, the administration unwittingly attracted enormous public suspicions of its intentions and objectives. Accordingly, we have experienced certain shortfalls and conflicting responses to the pulls and pushes of governance in the course of policy implementation.

I believe that areas of difficulties with the

transition programme, especially from the last quarter of 1992 to the recent cancelled presidential election, derived primarily from the shortfalls in implementing the programmes of actions which, though objectively taken, may have caused a deviation from the original framework and structure of the programme.

Fellow Nigerians, it is true that by the cancelled presidential election, we all found the nation at a peculiar bar of history which was neither bargained for, nor was it envisaged in the reform programmes of transition as enunciated in 1986/87. In the circumstance, the administration had no option than to respond appropriately to the unfortunate experience of terminating the presidential election. Our actions are in full conformity with the original objectives of the transition to civil programme. It was also in conformity with the avowed commitment of the administration to advance the cause of national unity, stability, and democracy. In annulling the presidential election, this administration was keenly aware of its promise in November 1992 that it would disengage and institute a return to democracy on August 27, 1993. We are determined to keep the promise.

Since this transition, and indeed any transition, must have an end, I believe that our transition programme should and must come to an end, honestly and honourably.

History will bear witness that as an administration we have always striven, in all our policy decisions, to build the foundation of lasting democracy. Lasting democracy is not a temporary show of excitement and manipulation by an over-articulate section of the elite and its captive audience; lasting democracy is a permanent diet to nurture the soul of the whole nation and the political process.

Therefore, it is logical, as we have always insisted upon, that lasting democracy must be equated with political stability.

Informed by our sad experience of history, we require nothing short of a foundation for lasting democracy. As an administration, we cannot afford to leave Nigerian into a Third Republic with epileptic convulsions in its democratic health. Nigeria must therefore confront her own reality; she must solve her problems notwithstanding other existing models of democracy in other parts of the world.

In my address to the nation in October 1992, when the first presidential primaries were cancelled, I had cause to remind our country men and women that there is nowhere in the world in which the practice of democracy is the same, even if the principles are similar and even for countries sharing the same intellectual tradition and cultural foundation. The history of our country is not the history of any other country in the world which is either practicing advanced democracy or struggling to lay the foundation for democracy. Yet, in spite of the uniqueness and peculiarities of Nigeria, there are certain prerequisites which constitute an irreducible minimum for democracy. Such essential factors include:

- A. Free and fair elections;
- B. Uncoerced expression of voters preference in election;
- C. Respect for electorate as unfettered final arbiter on elections;
- D. Decorum and fairness on the part of the electoral umpires;
- E. Absolute respect for the rule of law.

Fellow Nigerians, you would recall that it was precisely because the presidential primaries of last year did not meet the basic requirements of free and fair election that the Armed Forces Ruling Council had good reason to cancel those primaries. The recently annulled presidential election was similarly afflicted by these problems.

Even before the presidential elections, and indeed at the party conventions, we had full knowledge of the bad signals pertaining to the enormous breach of the rules and regulations of democracy elections. But because we were determined to keep faith with the deadline of 27th August 1993 for the return of civil rule, we overlooked the reported breaches. Unfortunately, these breaches continued into the presidential election of June 12, 1993, on an even greater proportion.

There were allegations of irregularities and other acts of bad conduct leveled against the presidential candidates but NEC went ahead and cleared them. There were proofs as well as documented evidence of widespread use of money during the party primaries as well as the presidential election. These were the same bad conduct for which the party presidential primaries of 1992 were cancelled.

Evidence available to government put the total amount of money spent by the presidential candidates as over two billion, one hundred million naira (N2.1 billion). The use of money was again the major source of undermining the electoral process.

Both these allegations and evidence were known to the National Defence and Security Council before the holding of the June 12, 1993 election, the National Defence and Security Council overlooked these areas of problems in its determination to fulfill the promise to hand over to an elected president on due date.

Apart from the tremendous negative use of money during the party primaries and presidential elections, there were moral issues which were also overlooked by the Defence and National Security Council. There were cases of documented and confirmed conflict of interest between the government and both presidential aspirants which would compromise their positions and responsibilities were they to become president. We believe that politics and government are not ends in themselves. Rather, service and effective amelioration of the condition of our people must remain the true purpose of politics.

It is true that the presidential election was generally seen to be free, fair and peaceful. However, there was in fact a huge array of election malpractices virtually in all the states of the federation before the actual voting began. There were authenticated reports of the election malpractices against party agents, officials of the National Electoral Commission and also some members of the electorate.

If all of these were clear violations of the electoral law there were proofs of manipulations through offer and acceptance of money and other forms of inducement against officials of the National Electoral Commission and members of the electorate. There were also evidence of conflict in the process of authentication and clearance of credentials of the presidential candidates. Indeed, up to the last few hours to the election, we continued in our earnest steadfastness with our transition deadline, to overlook vital facts.

For example, following the council's deliberation which followed the court injunction suspending the election, majority of members of the National Defence and Security Council supported postponement of the election by one week. This was to allow NEC enough time to reach all the voters, especially in the rural areas, about the postponement. But persuaded by NEC that it was capable of relaying the information to the entire electorate within the few hours left before the election, the council, unfortunately, dropped the idea of shifting the voting day. Now, we know better. The conduct of the election, the behaviour of the candidates and post-election responses continued to elicit signals which the nation can only ignore at its peril.

It is against the foregoing background that the administration became highly concerned when these political conflicts and breaches were carried to the court.

It must be acknowledged that the performance of the judiciary on this occasion was less than satisfactory. The judiciary has been the bastion of the hopes and liberties of our citizens.

Therefore, when it became clear that the courts had become intimidated and subjected to the manipulation of the political process, and vested interests then the entire political system was in clear dangers.

This administration could not continue to watch the various high courts carry on their long drawn out processes and contradictory decisions while the nation slides into chaos.

It was under this circumstance that the National Defence and Security Council decided that it is in the supreme interest of law and order, political stability and peace that the presidential election be annulled. As an administration, we have had special interest and concern not only for the immediate needs of our society, but also in laying the foundation for generations to come.

To continue action on the basis of the June 12, 1993 election, and to proclaim and swear in a president who encouraged a campaign of divide and rule among our ethnic groups would have been detrimental to the survival of the Third Republic. Our need is for peace, stability and continuity of politics in the interest of all our people.

Fellow countrymen and women, although the National Electoral Commission and the Centre for Democratic Studies officially invited foreign observers for the presidential elections, the administration also considered it as important as a democratic society, that our activities and electoral conduct must be open not only to the citizenry of our country but also to the rest of the world. In spite of this commitment, the administration did not and cannot accept that foreign countries should interfere in our internal affairs and undermine our sovereignty.

The presidential election was no an exercise imposed on Nigerians by the United Nations or by the wishes of some global policemen of democracy. It was a decision embarked upon independently by the government of our country and for the interest of our country. This is because, we believe, just like other countries, that democracy and democratization are primary values which Nigerians should cultivate, sustain and consolidate so as to enhance freedom, liberties and social development of the citizenry.

The actions of these foreign countries are most unfortunate and highly regrettable. There is nowhere in the history of our country or indeed of the third world where these countries can be said to love Nigeria or Nigerians any more that the love we have for ourselves and for our country. Neither can they claim to love Nigeria any more than this administration loves our country.

Accordingly, I wish to state that this administration will take necessary action against any interest groups that seek to interfere in our internal affairs. In this vein, I wish to place on record the appreciation of this administration for the patience and understanding of Nigerians, the French, the Germans, the Russians and Irish governments in the current situation. I appeal to our fellow countrymen and women and indeed our foreign detractors that they should cultivate proper understanding and appreciation of the peculiar historic circumstances in the development of our country and the determination not only of this administration but indeed of all Nigerians to resolve the current crises.

Fellow Nigerians, the National Security and Defence Council have met several times since the June 12, 1993 election. The council has fully deliberated not only on our avowed commitment but also to bequeathing to posterity, a sound economic and political base in our country and we shall do so with honour. In our deliberations, we have also taken note of several extensive consultations with other members of this administration, with officers and men of the Armed Forces and will well-meaning Nigerian leaders of thought. We are committed to handing over power on 27th August 1993.

Accordingly, the National Defence and Security Council has decided that by the end of July 1993 the two political parties, under the supervision of a recomposed National Electoral Commission, will put in place the necessary process for the emergence of two presidential candidates.

This shall be conducted according to the rules and regulations governing the election of the president of the country. In this connection, government will in consultation with the two political parties and National Electoral Commission agree as to the best and quickest process of conducting the election.

In the light of our recent experience and, given the mood of the nation, the National Defence and Security Council has imposed additional conditions as a way of widening and deepening the base of electing the president and sanitizing the electoral process. Accordingly, the candidates for the coming election must:

(1) Not be less than 50 years old.

(2) Have not been convicted of any crime;

(3) Believe, by act of faith and practice, in the corporate existence of Nigerians;

(4) Posses records of personal, corporate and business interests which do not conflict with the national interests;

(5) Have been registered members of either of the two political parties for at least one year to this election.

All those previously banned from participating in the transition process other than those with criminal records, are hereby unbanned. They can all henceforth participate in the electoral process. This is with a view to enriching the quality of candidature for the election and at the same time tap the leadership resources of our country to the fullest. The decree to this effect will be promulgated.

Fellow Nigerians, I wish to finally acknowledge the tremendous value of your patience and understanding, especially in the face of national provocation.

I urge you to keep faith with the commitment of this administration.

I enjoin you to keep faith with the unity, peace and stability of our country for this is the only country that you and I can call our own. Nowhere in the world, no matter the prompting and inducements of foreign countries, can Nigerians ever be regarded as first class citizens. Nigeria is the only country that we have. We must therefore renew our hope in Nigeria, and faith and confidence in ourselves for continued growth, development and progress.

Thank you all, and God bless you.

11

Anatomy of Public-Fund Looting: The Speaker Who Came, Saw, and Squandered

——————————◆——————————

■ Then, of course, there's the matter of Etteh's lazy tongue. Her accent, a combination of adulterated grammar and backwoods vernacular, made her the laughing stock among House members as she could not make a sentence without butchering the language. For instance, she shocked the audience when she was giving a vote of thanks to some visiting European Diplomats, saying, "We are happy to received the strangers in our midst."

——————————◆——————————

I despise public officers who prey on tax-payers' money, or public funds of any sort, and that is why, if I were the great Biblical Judge, King Solomon, and had disgraced Texas Southern University ex-president, Priscilla Slade [1-p.165] sitting on the dock as a defendant, I would slam her with 10

■ WHAT A MESS…. **Patricia Olubunmi Etteh** assumed the position of the first female Speaker of the House of Representatives in Nigeria, Africa's most populous country, on June 5, 2007 - then she was booted in less than four months, amidst accusations of embezzlement and corruption.

years on each of the two charges leveled against her, to run concurrently. I would also rule that after serving her prison term, she should be extradited to Timbuktu, the historical slave town, for a lifetime community service cleaning public toilets and sweeping un-tarred streets. Unfortunately I can't be a judge. I don't think anybody would have even let me into that jury box on Slade because I would come with a machete.

But wait a minute. Slade may attain sainthood if put side-by-side with another sister who similarly disgraced her constituency, and in fact let down the entire country. Patricia Olubunmi Etteh assumed the position of the first female Speaker of the House of Representatives in Nigeria, Africa's most populous country, on June 5, 2007. But then she was booted less than four months after, amidst accusations of embezzlement and corruption. Though Slade earned this reputation for fiscal irresponsibility, her alleged fund-misappropriation spread out over seven years she was in office. But Etteh's public-fund assault lasted for just three months, incurring a kind of damage that left political writers and the entire world aghast. She had misappropriated approximately $5 million in only three months of office.

Soon after this woman took office, she gave herself over to unbridled insanity, staging elaborate parties in cities in Europe, United States, and Canada. She approved thousands of dollars

(1) **Page 163** - In March, 2008, **TSU's Slade** avoided prison with a plea deal. A scandal that began in 2006 when a TSU regent complimented Priscilla Slade's choice of home furnishings ended Wednesday with a deal that lets the ousted leader of Texas' largest historically black university avoid prison in exchange for paying back $127,672.18. Nonpayment of restitution would be a violation of her probation. She must also perform 400 hours of community service *(Chron.com)*.

for lavish oversea trips and told her country she had gone away for a medical check-up. Medical check-up? To my knowledge, when she visited Houston, she never made it to the Medical Center, but she did manage to shuttle herself between banks, malls, and private parties which she hosted.

Just like Slade, Etteh, in her insatiable appetite for public fund embezzlement, approved huge contracts for companies she allegedly arranged to renovate her official residence, without due process. By law, for such contracts, newspaper advertisements ought to have been published for two weeks. This is the same fair bidding process Slade was alleged to have evaded in her contract-awarding mess during her tenure.

According to *International Guardian,* Etteh did even worse damage, distributing more than $5 million to over-inflated contracts. She awarded $239,000 for the installation of CCTV and multiple intercom systems in her private residence; a project appraised at just $40,000. The Honorable Speaker additionally spent a whopping $80,000 on a walk-through metal detector in her residence. A gadget which normally costs $15,000. In summary, Etteh was accused of allocating a hefty sum of over $5 million just to furnish her house and that of her deputy, and to purchase a fleet of cars including; 8 Toyota Land Cruisers, 4 Toyota Jeeps, 4 Peugeot 406s and 2 Mercedes Benz 500s.

Etteh specifically approved half a million dollars to personal home furnishings, making Slade look like a thrifty spender. In this case, comparably, Slade may be qualified for sainthood. It can be recalled that Slade specifically was accused of an unauthorized spending of $87,000 to furnish her home, $138,000 on landscaping and exterior improvements, and $56,000 on security related equipment and labor. She reimbursed some of the money, citing "over-sight" as an excuse for using school's money for landscaping.

Slade spent nearly $650,000 during the past seven years on personal purchases not allowed under her contract. Some of that was tuition money. Consequently, Slade used tuition or state money to buy music CDs, concert tickets and other items for her church ($7,420); and Christmas gifts for university board members and other executive staff ($16,963). As if this were not enough, she spent $143,636 for full-time maid service, about $28,000 for fixing up a former home, $154,528 for home furnishings and $48,363 for china, crystal and other serving pieces from Neiman Marcus, according to the audit.

As of her exit, Etteh remained the most notorious gold-digger, appearing in every media headline. But the militant Nigerian media did not back down, as headlines and kickers bludgeoned the disgraced speaker to pitiful ignominy.

Etteh is no Martha Stewart[1] by any stretch of the imagination, especially when placed between Slade and former Metro's boss, Shirley DeLibero [2] in an executive misconduct line-up. Based on her brazen administrative indiscretions, one could easily mistake her for the high-dollar providers bartering their services on Craig's List of erotic service providers.

Mrs. Etteh was born August 17, 1954 to the family of Alabi in Ikire, Osun State. She was married to an Oyo-based architect,

(1) Martha Stewart was a multimillionaire businesswoman who was sentenced July, 2004, to five months in prison for obstructing a federal securities investigation, then marched outside the courthouse to declare that "a small personal matter" had been blown out of proportion and urged supporters to stick with her company's products.

(2) Shirley DeLibero was the president of Houston's Metropolitan Transit Authority, in the year 2000, who admitted, among other transgressions, that she padded her resume. She sought forgiveness from her employers, saying she never intended to deceive people about her education.

Etteh Etteh, for whom she had two children. But the honorable speaker had since abandoned her husband without an official divorce, and spent her time flirting with high-powered politicians who took her on rally-trips, vacations, and secret escapades. In fact, the speaker didn't bring any of her family members the day she was sworn in, fueling speculation of her deteriorating marital status.

She had her early education at Baptist Primary School, Surulere, Ilorin in Kwara State where she obtained her Primary School Leaving Certificate in 1961, after which she proceeded to Aiyedade Grammar School, Ikire, between 1968 to 1973, for her Secondary School Certificate. Now, these were the only documented academic achievements of this troubled dame, as far as paper-evidence is concerned. Though she claimed to have gone to London's Morris School of Beauty in 1975 and London College of Modeling in 1976, verification remains a mystery. In fact, critics at the time said these schools did not appear on any lists of accredited European vocational schools.

Then, of course, there's the matter of Etteh's lazy tongue. Her accent, a combination of adulterated grammar and backwoods vernacular made her the laughing stock among House members as she could not make a sentence without butchering the language. For instance, she shocked the audience when she was giving a vote of thanks to some visiting European Diplomats, saying, "We are happy to received the strangers in our midst." In another occasion, she pleaded with a road management agency to "please make our roads habitable."

Etteh's human resources file is filled with fabricated paperwork. Those familiar with her story understood perfectly well that she was one of the dirty dozen who fraudulently made it to the top. Between 1999-2003, she hustled her way into the University of Abuja for a questionable part-time program and walked out with a diploma in Law. The last time I googled her, she had posted a Bachelors of Science degree in political science from the same institution - all of a sudden.

Everything about her shady academic claims and political timeline stank: it simply reeked of deceit. Etteh was first elected to the House in 1999 on the platform of Alliance for Democracy (AD), which, immediately, selected her as its Chief Whip. During the same period, she was already handling former Nigerian president behind closed doors, and by 2002, Etteh decamped to the ruling People's Democratic Party, on whose platform she was re-elected to the House in 2003. Oddly enough, this was exactly the same period she got all her academic degrees - and I'm sure they weren't on-line

12

The Gospel according to Frank Nweke Jr.

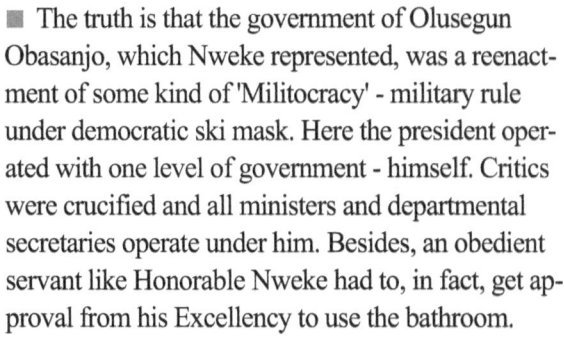

■ The truth is that the government of Olusegun Obasanjo, which Nweke represented, was a reenactment of some kind of 'Militocracy' - military rule under democratic ski mask. Here the president operated with one level of government - himself. Critics were crucified and all ministers and departmental secretaries operate under him. Besides, an obedient servant like Honorable Nweke had to, in fact, get approval from his Excellency to use the bathroom.

Patriotism is not an invalid inference. It is love and devotion to one's country. For one reason, according to Lord Lytton, "every man loves and admires his own country because it produced him." Even Theodore Roosevelt was not left out in some encouraging definition of this 10-letter word, in way of boosting a spirit of unconditional love for ones country. According to him, "The man who loves other countries as much as he loves his own is like the man who loves other women as

■ **Wrong Gospel**... besides, an obedient servant like **Honorable Minister Frank Nweke Jr.** has to, in fact, get approval from his **Excellency, President Obasanjo** (inset) to use the bathroom.

much as he loves his own wife." However, just like love, patriotism is a two-way street and thrives most in a country that shows love and respect for her masses.

This explains why love sometimes revolts - out of betrayal or unbearable abuse. When Nigeria's Minister of Information and Communication, under the Olusegun Obasanjo regime, The Honorable Frank Nweke Jr. breezed into Houston on a late

February, in 2007, he came to market a project; his project he dubbed "The Heart of Africa" conference, which is clearly a public relation blitz to showcase his country's businesses, products, people, sports, culture and cities - to the world.

But this man knew there was nothing unique about his mission. His predecessors had invested millions in such ventures in the past without a single positive result. So Nweke came prepared with a defense. It was more of a gospel that preaches patriotism but counters questions about the chaotic nature of the present socio-political structure of the country; questions about lack of security that was at the time threatening investment; questions about corruption among the leadership class; questions about political instability, and questions about abundant oil revenue and yet no amenities. All such questions the minister categorized as unnecessary propaganda by CNN and unpatriotic Nigerians in the Diaspora.

The minister's campaign was clouded with bitterness over a CNN report about instability in Nigeria's Niger Delta, even accusing them of paying masked militants for the story piece. CNN flatly denied the charge and sent a letter to Nweke asking him to provide any evidence to support his claims. If any credible evidence was forthcoming, CNN said it would report on that. Nweke never did. The *Nigerian Guardian* believed that there was nothing new about CNN's report . It was right. It wrote, "Really, there is little the CNN revealed that is not already public knowledge here and elsewhere, that has not been expressed one way or another by Nigerians themselves, especially those who suffer the realities in the Niger Delta." Also, CNN's Jeff Koinange said he was in Abuja, Nigeria's capital for five days trying to get the government's input on the story but to no avail.

I believed him so well because, this was the same period, mid-January, I made my trip to Nigeria working on a similar

■ These are EMPTY SEATS, four hours into **Honorable Minister Nweke's** "Heart of Africa" conference, in Stafford, outskirt of Houston, Texas. Nigerians knew the senselessness in such a lavish public relation blitz. *photo/International Guardian.*

story on both insecurity in that region and assault on the tax payers but could not get any government official to talk to me. In fact, a staff of the Ministry of Information categorically told me after interrogating me with irrelevant questions, "We don't talk to press." I am familiar with journalism in Nigeria and understand both the system and government's position when it comes to free press. Media freedom in this region is like women freedom under the Taliban.

The truth is that the government of Olusegun Obasanjo, which Nweke represented, was a reenactment of some kind of 'militocracy,' representing military rule under democratic ski mask. Here the president operated with one level of government - himself. Critics were crucified and all ministers and departmental secretaries operate under him. Besides, an obedient servant like Honorable Nweke had to, in fact, get approval from his Excellency to use the bathroom.

I was disturbed by the irony of this man, who is committed to a pricey worldwide media campaign to save the image of a regime that chastises the media with acid. Just about then, Nigerian journalists were thrown into massive mourning when one of their own, Mr. Godwin Agbroko, was shot dead by unknown vandals. The police said armed robbers shot Agbroko, but the family claimed he was murdered. No surprise, Agbroko was the chairman of the Editorial Board of *This Day*, one of Nigeria's outspoken daily publications.

Early January, 2007, about the same period - an early morning fire reduced the fourth floor of *This Day's* Lagos corporate office to smoldering ashes. Britain, through its High Commissioner to Nigeria, Richard Gozney, expressed concern over press freedom in Nigeria so close to an April's landmark elections, citing the detention of four newspaper editors and the unsolved killing of Agbroko in Lagos.

The State Security Services (SSS) detained two editors from *Leadership* newspaper and two from the *Abuja Inquirer* on January 9 and 10 over political articles. They were freed within days but were still under investigation and intimidation by the SSS.

It may not be easy to say this, but I really think that Nweke's "Heart of Africa" campaign was a daylight scam. Mouth-running at noisy hotel conferences full of lobbyists and shabby Art exhibitions were an erroneous portrayal of the most populous country in Africa. No doubt - this country called Nigeria is great and Nweke needn't tell me that. Nigeria remains the United States' largest trading partner after the United Kingdom, a key member of the Organization of Petroleum Exporting Countries (OPEC), with proven oil reserves estimated to be more than 25 billion barrels, and natural gas reserves over 100 trillion cubic feet. Nigeria, with its ravaged image, does not need cosmetic propaganda by any team of dollar-gulping damage control experts. No! They need honest leaders to clean the filth from the top. They need an independent legislative and judicial arm to do their jobs without retaliatory consequences perpetrated by the executive arm.

I'm sure that the honorable minister understands where I'm coming from. If not, how could anybody hope to sanitize a country where the two highest ranking officers, the president and the vice are scandalously drowning in a deep sea of indictments over open-day public money embezzlement?

It was disappointing that Honorable Nweke did not know this, but thieves stay in jailhouses, not in government offices. It is a fact that in the same week, the All Nigerian Peoples Party (ANPP) called on both President Obasanjo and Vice President Abubakar to resign from office for "denigrating the institution of the Presidency." The report of the Senate Committee on Petroleum Technology Development Fund (PTDF) had, indicted Vice President Abubakar of diversion of public fund and blamed President Obasanjo for approving money for some projects before the Federal Executive Council endorsed them. What a shame!

I had quickly recommended in an *International Guardian* editorial, that the foreign embassies, especially those of America and Europe, should reverse their policies and slow down issuance of travel visas to African public officers, unless their missions were genuine and well-documented. This simple method would pragmatically frustrate the exportation of taxpayer's money from African countries to western financial institutions..

13

Repressive Nigerian Leaders and the Fire in Holy Ghost Fire

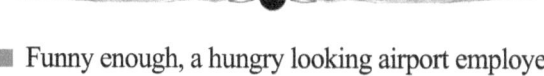

■ Funny enough, a hungry looking airport employee who took bribe from me at the Lagos domestic airport not only told me that 'God will Bless' me, but also, the fool turned around and asked me where I would worship that Sunday. He knew virtually all churches, and called their pastors by their first names. He invited me to his church, and in an insatiable tone said, "Bring me something when you come O oga."

Besides soil soaked in dollar-yielding quality crude, there is one more endowment bequeathed by Mother Nature to Nigeria - the rich and powerful Africa's giant - and this is spiritual prowess exercised by acclaimed prayer merchants representing God's mission on earth.

My 2006 visit to Nigeria saw a growing number of churches, scattered at all corners of the streets. In fact, almost every street has a church in any major city and an average citizen claims to be a "born again" - term used by Christians for those who have given their lives to Christ in fulfillment of a revelation in the *Book of John (3)* that " unless one is born again, he cannot see the kingdom of God." It was a culture of sorts, because even rogues, motor park purse-snatchers, kidnappers, and those corrupt public officers would always tell you, "To God Be The Glory," before shaking your hands or even before stealing from you.

Funny enough, a hungry looking airport employee who took bribe from me at the Lagos domestic airport not only told me that 'God will Bless' me, but also, the fool turned around and asked me where I would worship that Sunday. He knew virtually all churches, and called their pastors by their first names. He invited me to his church, and in an insatiable tone said, "Bring me something when you come O oga." This is just Nigeria, and how far the citizens have gone to embrace powers other than the coercive authorities of their leaders.

Hence, Nigerian Christians do not play when it comes to deliverance in the form of dry fasting and intensive prayers as panacea for a nation devastated by corruption championed by her trusted leaders. This is a nation where the rich flourish on stolen fund from tax-payers, and where the national anthem has been replaced with cries of frustration and anxiety prompted by near perpetual austerity. But despite this catastrophe, dependability on their faith and trust in God by these believers have gotten conspicuously powerful.

In Nigeria, prayer merchants, and the so-called believers consistently maintain their spiritual communication with the Almighty, as a tool for bringing defiant and wicked leaders to book and this appears to be working. It seems so coincidental, but events showed that Nigerian leaders who defied warnings by prayerful Christians and proceeded with punitive strategies against defenseless Nigerian masses failed woefully as maintained by these God's servants according to the Holy *Book of Psalm* that "the way of the ungodly shall perish."

Nigerians started realizing the spiritually-coded powers of these churches and their intercessors after the death of one of its presidents, General Abacha, who, of course was rated one of the country's most dangerous leader since its independence in 1960. He had taken over from his predecessor, former military leader, Ibrahim Babangida.

General Babangida was forced to resign by mounting pressure over oppression and elections violations, but things got worse as Abacha, who assumed leadership refused to address a hand over to a democratically elected regime.

When matters came to a head, Nigerian Christians issued an ultimatum. God's followers, including a Lagos-based church with branches all over the world declared a three-day prayer period and dry fasting in the country. It was like a convention. It was not really a moment of revenge or antagonism against the Country's leadership, but a call to God to take control and come to the aid of millions of defenseless populace as witnessed in the Book of *Psalm (72)* that 'He will deliver the needy when he cries, The Poor also, and him who has no helper."

The last day of this prayer declaration was an outright spiritual warfare - a combination of screams of Holy Ghost Fire, and Hallelujah took the air as these warriors spoke in tongue, asking God to save the country from disaster. By daybreak, president Abacha was pronounced dead. He died in his sleep, without prior health problems. The visit of late Pope John Paul II to Nigeria prior to this final event, it was also gathered, may have neutralized all supernatural powers that guided Abacha's evil deeds, thereby opening him up for impending repercussions. The Pontiff, it was gathered looked Abacha in the eyes and shook hands with him. Those close to the General revealed that since this handshake, Abacha was never the same till his controversial death.

Abacha was not the first victim of his deeds. In mid eighties, another leader - a governor who chastised the masses got what he wanted. Lagos State Governor Raji Rasaki once went on rampage and demolished thousands of houses in swampy area of Maroko where the low class dwelled. He wanted that area situated near the oceanfront for the top army generals, including him, so he sent rightful owners parking without compensation.

To make matters worse, he served a church pastored by one young Man of God with a quit notice because a Muslim associate did not want a church in that neighborhood. Rasaki's Muslim associate had also complained about the distraction of seeing a cross or a church anytime he came out to pray. Treading on the cross was where Governor Rasaki crossed the line.

Christian merchants went into fasting and endless prayers. They had relied on the Book of *First Peter* that questions, "Who is he who will harm you if you become followers of what is good?" They didn't mean revenge, but only raised hands in the air to follow orders from the Book of *Psalm,* "Praising God in His Sanctuary and Praising Him in His Mighty Firmament." They strongly professed the Book of *Proverb (18)* that "the name of God is a strong tower," and that "the righteous run to it and are safe." By the end of this revival, Rasaki's problems began. First - his wife died mysteriously with his two sons in a ghastly car wreck, and the rest is history. The church went further to observe a moment of silence for the late First Lady, with a short phrase by the Pastor that "God works in a mysterious way - Amen." More than two decades since this incident,

Rasaki had battled to regain a political balance, falling from one mysterious problem or the other.

Even, one of Nigeria's longest serving military leaders, Ibrahim Babangida - who is now enjoying his loots of public treasury - had an experience with repercussions from his stewardship. He had defied warnings by the Christian community about falsely portraying Nigeria as a Muslim State. This was also in the eighties. He had actualized Nigeria's membership of the Organization of Islamic Cooperation (OIC); a move Nigerian Christians saw as a relegation of the country's secularity.

Christians raised hands and prayed for IBB for repentance. Ironically, the stubborn general ended up on a hospital bed in France, diagnosed with radiculopathy - a muscle and bone related infection that almost ended his leadership career." That was not all; IBB witnessed one after the other, numerous plagues that shadowed his regime, facing off with economic hardship that defied all money management theories. He rode his economic train from Austerity Measures to Structural Adjustment Program, faced severe socio-political crisis until he resigned from this position. He miraculously became the first Nigeria's military leader to give up a presidential position out of severe pressure.

Spiritual warfare in Africa's most populous country got pronounced attention, especially after the death of the country's First lady, Stella Obasanjo. Stella had gone on rampage using unspecified names to acquire government properties and corporations. Before she met her final demise in an operating room in Spain, 2005, she had acquired a residential estate (called '1,004 flats') occupied mainly by the middle class; and she had issued a quit notice to these defenseless occupants. Three notable churches whose members reside in this estate went into a

■ Spiritual warfare in Africa's most populous country got pronounced attention, especially after the death of the country's First lady, **Stella Obasanjo** who had gone on rampage using unspecified names to acquire government properties and corporations.

non-stop prayer revival. All they asked God was a shelter and protection among His children as proclaimed in *The Book of Ezekiel, 43,* that "they shall no more be a threat to the heathen, neither shall the beast of the land devour them, but they shall dwell safely and non shall make them afraid." Stella died in the operating room after a cosmetic surgery.

Nigerian Christians are often fearless and more effective than the media when it comes to demand for righteousness, fairness and thoroughness in leadership. Broken into denominations with churches and cathedrals scattering in every corners of the country's townships, ousting of corrupt and wicked leaders or using prayers to influence damaging proposals are automatically within their control.

IV

CLOSING THOUGHTS

14

Final Thoughts

> ■ Nigeria's power structure was deceptively not built to last. The complexity of its leadership structure is an off-shoot of a misguided experiment by the colonial government. No leadership paradigm thrives within a domain of incompatible cultural values where stakeholders are indoctrinated an awful irreconcilable ideologies that undermine unity and cordiality; yet Nigeria parades as her motto "Unity and Faith".

There are reasons why Post-Impressionist, Vincent Van Gogh and renaissance artist Leonardo Da Vinci would do a live painting capturing exactly the same subject, but rendering them in entirely different brush strokes. Both painters were inspired differently in such ways that cause them to react contrarily when demonstrating their emotions with brush-strokes and paints on canvas. Van Gogh began painting from memory, and this resulted in his works becoming more decorative and less accurate. Leonardo was largely inspired by nature, and this led him to study anatomy, geology, medicine, and other disciplines that are shown in his great works. So, Van Gogh was not over-reacting with a style of clashing and rioting brush strokes; he was simply telling his story his way, as directed by his emotion.

Psychology of emotions have always played a major role in the philosophical study of the structures of experience and consciousness. As a child victim of a devastating Nigeria's civil war genocide, and a sorry victim of a series of junta regimes, my tone of narratives in this book may be excused.

This pogrom has a significant effect on my reaction, or over-reaction toward concerns of Mother Land – Nigeria thus Africa, and these emotions may be explained and excused when narrators, reporters or storytellers are victims of specific traumatizing events, measures or processes. That, however, does not constitute distortion of realities or falsification of facts. It is simply, a composition method that brings out the truth with an attitude influenced by memories of specific occasions. In other words, the attitude may be different, or even strange, but the facts remain as pure as spring water.

By now, we may be in agreement that *336 Hours in Nigeria* is definitely not   a piece for the outdoor and tourism dispatch in a news journal, but a psychological composition of the suffering of a Nation fabricated for contingency, rather than built to last. What does this mean to an average Nigerian nursing hope of a united great nation?

It is simply an indication that any solution must start from addressing the mistakes of the founding fathers. Nigeria's power structure was deceptively not built to last. The complexity of its leadership structure is an offshoot of a misguided experiment by the colonial government. No leadership paradigm thrives within a domain of incompatible cultural values where

stakeholders are indoctrinated an awful irreconcilable ideologies that undermine unity and cordiality; yet Nigeria parades
as her motto "Unity and Faith". Which unity, and where is the
faith?

Some self-acclaimed Nigerian do-or-die patriots may not
agree, but Nigeria's current pitiful state is highly connected to
a lack of intellectual honesty of most of her leaders who
presided over a complex nation without adequate understanding
of leadership and all it surrounding contexts.

I have, in quest for issue identification and analysis, refer-
enced authentic occasions by specific past leaders, and scanned
them through Organizational Development and leadership theories to discover how the ideals of dictatorship could override
effective governance and ruin a nation, her people, and social,
political, and economic progress. Of course, it does bother
me that since her independence in 1960, only the late President
Yar'Adua, and current leader, President Jonathan are the only
heads of state with a basic college degree.

It may not sound strange enough, but the consequences are
an accumulation of policy failures that shape Nigeria's current
governance disaster. It may proper to go to school and acquire
formal knowledge before aspiring for leadership positions, but
it is despicable that in Nigeria, it is the other way round. For
instance, military leader, Yakubu Gowon, who ruled Nigeria
from 1966 to 1975 had to in fact go to college after he was
ousted. Another Junta, Ibrahim Babangida, who chastised
Nigeria from 1985 to 1993 had no college education, but acquired a trigger-by-trigger military training; and was able to in-
stigate the coups that ousted Gowon in 1975; Shagari in 1983,
and Buhari in 1985. Another junta, Sani Abacha (1993 1998)
who could not even pronounce his own policies equally played

a role in many military coups until he gatecrashed into leadership.

Some skeptics may again differ, but I postulated the deleterious impact of how as of this day, the Hausa Land now called Northern Nigeria has unforgivingly destabilized the secularity of Nigeria's nationhood by operating all the major Islamic standards as applies to the radical institution of their spiritual founding fathers. For instance, the Islamization of Nigeria's currency (Naira and Kobo); movement of Nigeria's capital city from west to the North; establishment of Sharia Court; forceful induction of Nigeria into the Organization of Islamic Conference; Introduction of Islamic Banking; Monopoly of political power, and so on are clear indication that the existence of Nigeria as a nation is a deceitful assumption that bear no hypothetical bearing.

From revelations, it is also clear that every Nigerian common citizen is a victim of any (if not all) of three major calamities; genocide, dictatorship, and economic predatory. Those born before July 6, 1967, may be categorized proud survivors of the civil war genocide; those born before March 20, 1984, proud survivors of Buhari's War Against Indiscipline (WAI), and those born before June 27, 1986, may be considered proud survivor of Babangida's' Structural Adjustment Programme (SAP).

Furthermore, it must be understood that patriotism as a Nigerian is not flying the national flag, or wearing designer suits adorned in green colors. It must not only be love for Nigeria, but also necessitates believing in those ideals that characterize her nationhood. Those who really love Nigeria are those citizens who believe that government should not sponsor pilgrimages and religious activities, including the Sharia laws. A true patriot would not endorse Nigeria's membership in Organization of the Islamic Conference (OIC), nor support military coups or any dictatorships as the best solutions to her democracy. No sensible patriotic Nigerian would endorse any of the Nigeria's past dictators, except those self-centered activists or sorry bootlickers who would fly the Nigerian flag only to seek positions and contracts, or other favors from unscrupulous public officers.

About the Author

■ Among his virtues is a rare combination of street and real-world smarts, and, even rarer among pen-wielding pros, he's unfailingly candid. As he readily confesses, he has no special powers that enable him to foretell the future, but he is sure to tell it like it is.

EMEABA EMEABA, PHD
(PUBLISHER, THE DRUM MAGAZINE)

It could be serendipitous, or that the planets were lined up correctly, but Ogbo got into the media circle in September 1981 as a student of Fine & Applied Arts. He became chief cartoonist of The Trumpet—a national weekly newspaper based in Eastern Nigeria, where he created the funny pages, and for three decades remained in mass media, changing both his education discipline, and professional portfolio along the way. Ogbo's job at The Trumpet then was a classic oxymoron—important but risky. He was in the business during that stormy political era of Nigeria's second republic in the early 80s, when killer thugs ran the society. Confessing, Ogbo says, "The instruction was to destabilize the local ruling party, the Nigerian People's Party, and deliver the state to the national ruling party, National Party of Nigeria. As a cartoonist, all I did was lampoon the opposition with destructive cartoon pieces. I shuttled between college, and newsroom... braved the chaotic environment to keep the momentum."

From The Trumpet, Ogbo moved to The *Daily Star,* then to The *Nigerian Guardian*, and *Prime People* magazine, all in Nigeria. When the media business became suicidal—the era of Ibrahim Babangida and his goons, exacerbated by a rundown economy, and a clash between the media and the military— Ogbo, whose irksome, controversially objective style of journalism had made headlines, and having been exposed to the real world of the print media, decided to move on. Even at the time in the Guardian, he doubled as a production supervisor in the operations section, and a cartoonist with the *Guardian Express* where he authored *Baba Toyin*—one of the most popular cartoon series at the time.

Coming to the U.S., Ogbo moved on to more serious stuff as Art director with the *Houston Sun*; Designer at the *Houston Chronicle*; and finally decided, if he could make others king, he could make himself king as well. Ogbo established his own business, and incorporated the Guardian Newspaper in 1998 with the sole purpose of serving a combination of African-American and African immigrants with information, and cultural matters. In 2008, he established a tabloid, The Black Senior News—readily the first publication in the State of Texas that addressed the needs of African-American seniors.

Among his virtues is a rare combination of street and real-world smarts, and, even rarer among pen-wielding pros, he's unfailingly candid. As he readily confesses, he has no special powers that enable him to foretell the future, but he is sure to tell it like it is.

Ogbo, who volunteers time to teaching and mentoring young African-American journalism students, was born of Igbo parentage in the ancient city of Kaduna in northern Nigeria. Now a US Citizen, Ogbo, a Texas-licensed private investigator, is a prominent member of the Nigerian expatriate Diaspora. He holds a degree in Fine & Applied Arts, Certificates in Commercial Arts, and Electronic Communication; a Masters in Human Resources and Human Resources Management, and a Doctorate in the esoteric field of Management in Organizational Leadership.

September 6, 2011, which was exactly 30 years since Ogbo dabbled in the print media, was proclaimed Anthony Obi Ogbo Day. Houston's Mayor Annise Parker's in the proclamation, wrote, "The City of Houston commends Anthony Ogbo Ogbo for his accomplishments and commitments to print media and community service."

Author's Quotes/Excerpts about Nigeria and Leadership

———◆———

■ I insist on my detestation of deadly fundamentalist, Boko Haram, and my unapologetic dislike of Central Bank Chief, Sanusi for bringing forth a religiously tailored banking system in a country where songs of sectarian lynching is like an anthem.

———◆———

PSYCHOLOGY OF LEADERSHIP IDENTITY

■ A man is known by the company he keeps (1912 'Saki' Chronicles of Clovis), therefore, I say, tell me your friend, and I will say who you are. For instance, Obama plays golf with Clinton, both are charismatic leaders; Romney dines with Trump, both are cruel capitalists; Mugabe worships Chavez, both are evil; Zuma hangs out with women, he is promiscuous; Jonathan hangs out with Gov. Dickson, both are brothers; Boko Haram worships Buhari, both are comrades.

PHILOSOPHY OF HISTORY AND ATTITUDE

■ "History has to be rewritten in every generation, because although the past does not change, the present does. Each generation asks new questions of the past, and finds new areas of sympathy as it re-lives different aspects of the experiences of its predecessors," (Christopher Hill). So my fellow Nigerians, when philosophers raise critical reflections about unforgotten gloomy side of our history, it does not mean that they hate their country; it does not signify a slur of a united Nation; it is simply a reminder to this nation that *"There Was a Country."*[1]

LEADERSHIP AND ETHICS

■ Moral philosophy refers to the principles, rules, and values people use in deciding what is right or wrong (Bateman–Snell). In other words, ethics is not necessarily what applies in our job responsibilities, or the constitution; it's not doing just what is right, but doing the right thing. Just yesterday, the Director of the Central Intelligence Agency Gen. David Petraeus, a retired four-star general who led the U.S. military campaigns in Iraq and Afghanistan, resigned from his post citing an extramarital affair. His words:

> "Yesterday afternoon, I went to the White House and asked the President to be allowed, for personal reasons, to resign from my position as D/CIA. After being married for over 37 years, I showed extremely poor judgment by engaging in an extramarital affair. Such behavior is unacceptable, both as a husband and as the leader of an organization such as ours. This afternoon, the President graciously accepted my resignation."

(1) *There Was a Country: A Personal History of Biafra* is **Chinua Achebe's** reminiscences on Biafra's short history, striking a surreally nostalgic and sentimental note.

Now, for those leaders and politicians who violate universal ethical values and wait for termination letter rather than an honorable departure, it is our responsibility to resist their stewardship.

DIVINE PSYCHOLOGY OF BROTHERHOOD

■ While Jesus was still addressing the crowd, his mother and brothers stood outside, wanting to speak to him. Someone told him, "Your mother and brothers are standing outside, wanting to speak to you." But Jesus replied, "Who is my mother, and who are my brothers?" Pointing to his disciples, he said, "Here are my mother and my brothers. For whoever does the will of my Father in heaven is my brother and sister and mother," (Matthew 12).

Therefore, our brother doesn't necessarily have to look like us, speak like us or share a DNA – he could be George Bush or even Mitt Romney; that is why Serena and Venus are our sisters, and Tiger Woods a pen pal.

LEADERSHIP LESSONS: THE FLOOD STORY

■ President of the United States of America, Barack Obama dwelled in the Situation Room directing safety and evacuation affairs even before a mean-hearted hurricane Sandy hit the American coasts. He had called off his campaign schedule in a presidential race less than 9 days away. Before the storm, Obama had ordered the coast guards to brace for a tough evacuation process; promised a swift federal action , and vowed to save lives even if it means "cutting through red tape."

Just last week, severe weathers dumped unimaginable waters in some parts of Nigeria causing extraordinary damages, with thousands of victims left without homes and possessions; unfortunately, there was no effective forecast apparatus to alert the people of imminent havoc. To deride the entire scenario, hopeless flood victims saw nothing but confused leaders who came after the storm, swimming in flood waters, paddling canoes and flying mini jets over disaster areas to fictitiously woo the media for photo opportunities.

May we remind us that leadership is not about winning elections; it is the ability to mitigate risks to protecting citizens, and saving lives. Official relief subsidies, sympathies, or swimming in floodwaters with victims are not leadership strategies; they are deceptive self-aggrandizement signifying 'medicine after death.'

THE AFRICAN CHILD...

■ And after their callous leaders cart away the whole resources, they would look at their victims and say, have hope, keep the faith, and follow your dreams: these are poor victims who don't even have a place to lay their heads. How can you dream if you don't sleep?

PSYCHOLOGY OF NATIVE LAND

■ With billions of assets hidden in foreign lands, overseas bank accounts, 'lying-lips,' and a hidden tax records, you don't need a birth certificate to figure out that this man called Romney is a corrupt African leader! Who knows? he may be related to former Nigeria's Delta State Governor, James Ibori.

CELEBRATING A DISSIDENT?

■ On July 29, 1975, Brigadier General Mohammed rebelled into power after a coup against General Gowon's regime. February 13, 1976, Murtala Mohammed was killed in a fruitless coup attempt led by Lt. Col Buka Suka Dimka. Dimka and other key officers who masterminded this Coup against Late General Mohammed's regime were sentenced to death which is an indication that it is treasonably illegal to overthrow a government. Since all these officers were guilty of the same offence, why honor and celebrate General Mohammed on the nation's currency? What would be his punishment for overthrowing Gowon's regime? What distinguishes Mohammed from IBB, Abacha and other inglorious juntas?

LEADERSHIP 101 FOR IDIOTS

■ President Obama and first lady Michelle Obama (United States) disclosed their assets recently. The Obamas hold the assets worth between nearly $2.6 million and nearly $8.3 million as per the reports released by the White House. President Obama believes it is the right thing to do, but President Jonathan of Nigeria says he doesn't "give a damn" about declaring his assets because the law says so. The critical question therefore, is how Jonathan's "damn" word and refusal to declare his possessions suit his presidential demeanor and transformational ideals.

Aristotle, the Greek philosopher, who taught Alexander the Great, explained that "We do not act rightly because we have virtue or excellence, but we rather have those because we have acted rightly." Warren Buffett shared a similar opinion, asserting that "Price is what you pay. Value is what you get." Consequently, Dwight David Eisenhower cautioned that, "A person that values its privileges above its principles soon loses both."

In transformational leadership which President Jonathan claims to execute, ethics is about doing the right thing not just following toe-to-toe what the law says. "Truly great companies are built on ideals, not just deals (Al Watts). Therefore, accountability is not the capacity not to embezzle; it is a demonstration, not a concealment of transparency. President Jonathan must adhere to the core demands of best practices in leadership process to redeem his latest directorial snafu. He must identify with the relevance of putting moral values before negligible theories.

NIGERIA: AIR SAFETY AND A CRYING PRESIDENT

■ Nigerians do not want to see their president cry at air crash scenes, but would want him to confront critical issues head-on with proven results. A crying attitude could translate to despair, hopelessness, and a lack of confidence over nerve-racking issues.

Organizational leadership is not disco – it is science, and operates with logical rules. As president, the core demands of executive control must also encompass the zeal to putting the country first, and the alluring attitude to protecting the lives of the citizens from hunger, diseases, and other vicious tragedies.

PSYCHOLOGY AND SPIRITUALITY

■ Just last week, this Nigerian preacher TB Joshua of The Synagogue Church said the death of an old African president was now very close. Reinstating his earlier prophecy that an old African president will die soon, Joshua hinted that the president will not be from West Africa. He spoke from his church in Nigeria exactly on Sunday, April 1, 2012. Today, Friday April 6, Malawi's president, Bingu wa Mutharika was reported dead. Doctors said that Mutharika, 78, died Thursday in Malawi of a heart attack. Now, any thoughts about the mystery of prophetic authority? Can the study of knowledge explain the vagueness in spiritual psychology?

THE GATES ARE A GOD-SENT

■ When God Blessed the Gates family, they did not think first about acquiring Gulf Stream private jets, Rolls Royce, Bentley or a Gulf Course in the Pacific Ocean – They dedicated their proceeds to enhance healthcare, reduce extreme poverty, expand educational opportunities, and access to information technology in the globe. Thus The Bill & Melinda Gates Foundation founded by Bill and

Melinda Gates remain the largest transparently operated private foundation in the world.

This is how you know a Messiah: this is how you know true servants of God. A God-sent or anointed servant does not amass wealth from a vulnerable flock and fly private jets over their heads or above the same domain devastated by disease, starvation and natural disasters. This is why any African-born pastor, or clergy, or minister engaged in this glitzy lifestyle of Rolls and private jets contests is not of God, but a dishonorable descendant of the Wall Street Evil – a culture of Money, Money and Money.

UNFINISHED WAR

■ Those fools who think Nigerian Civil War ended 1970 must answer some philosophical questions: why was the currency changed from Pound and Shillings to Naira and Kobo? What is Kobo? Why was the capital moved from LAGOS to ABUJA? Why were trillions invested in moving the crude from South-South to the North? My friends, a slave who does not know he is a slave can never inhale freedom.

ISLAMIC BANKING

■ I insist on my detestation of deadly fundamentalist like Boko Haram, and my unapologetic dislike of Central Bank Chief, Sanusi for bringing forth a religiously tailored banking system in a country where songs of sectarian lynching is like an anthem.

PSYCHOLOGY OF SELF-DENIAL

■ Let's face the facts and quit the pretense. You cannot be an advocate of one Nigeria, and want Islamic or Christian Redeemed banking; You cannot be asking for a peacefully united Nigeria, and be advocating peace or friendship with Boko. You cannot claim to be a secular nation and occupy a front seat in Organization of Islamic Conference. Consequently, you cannot eat your cake, wash it down with orange juice, and then want it back!!!

BATTLELINE

■ Get it clear – that the war for social justice and economic prosperity in Nigeria is not 'us versus us'… it's between us versus the leadership. Therefore, we must unite, and hold all our leaders - past and present responsible for our past, present, and future.

NIGERIA'S LEADERS

■ Since independence in 1960, Nigeria has been ruled by only three categories of leaders - Just three not four. Those who stole themselves to power through election rigging; those who got legitimately elected in a fair but imperfect election process, and those who gate-crashed into leadership in smutty camouflaged khaki and ruled with empty brains and loaded rifles.

WHY WE ARE WHERE WE ARE

■ Leadership is a complex phenomenon involving the constant interaction of three essential elements: the leader, the followers, and the surrounding situation or context" (J. Thomas Warren). What happens then, where the leadership process serves only the interest of a few unscrupulous leaders, at the detriment of the followers, and surrounding circumstance?

THREE ARMS

■ Goodluck Jonathan has now been sworn in today – therefore it has become official that Nigeria now has an Executive Branch. So, when are we going to have a Legislative Branch, and Judiciary?

ALLAH DOES NOT NEED KILLER-THUGS

■ The tendency to claim God as an ally for our partisan value and ends is the source of all religious fanaticism (Reinhold Niebuhr). Those Muslims who kill, destroy properties in name of Allah, or in defense of Muslim values are not from Allah; they are ill-informed hooligans disorganized about life, and distressed by ignorance of faith and spirituality. God does not need killer-tugs and bodyguards; He is the Almighty and can take care of every business.

EVERY VOTE COUNTS

■ Ongoing campaign to return Obama to office is not just an affair for democrats; it's a global call to move the United States, and the world forward. Everybody must go to the polls now and November 6 too. if you are not an American, just go to sleep and vote Obama in your dreams; all votes count!!!

PSYCHOLOGY OF COMMONSENSE

■ Texas, a predominantly energy state, is the second most populous and the second most extensive of the 50 states in the United States of America. She is the most extensive state of the 48 contiguous United States. With an area of 268,820 square miles (696,200 km2), and a growing population of 25.7 million residents, the state swanks an $80.6 billion budget for FY2012-13.

Unlike some Nigerian governors, it may interest you to know that the governor of Texas, Rick Perry does not own a private jet; he does not own a state-owned 'personally' assigned official luxury jet, and he does not own a private foreign account either. Therefore I am saying to us - the more we defend those leaders stealing our economic fortune, the more our nation dwindles in disgraceful impoverishment.

Islamic economics 101

■ Nigeria's Central Bank Chief, Sanusi says his Islamic Bank will not discriminate. Unlawful Discrimination is an injurious or arbitrary treatment of people on the grounds of race, age, sex, religion, gender, ancestry, disability status, and so on. Islam forbids pigs, so if a farmer is denied a loan for his piggery by an Islamic bank, wouldn't that be discriminatory?

■ As a victim of Nigerian Civil War, I saw sectarian brutality in the pre-combat campaign; I have observed Nigeria's OIC membership process, and I am yet to see any benefits besides support for Boko Haram through Iran, Al-Qaeda, Hamas, and Taliban - so at this juncture, I really do not need to listen to those illogical tommyrots in support of Islamic Banking. I bank Morgan Chase in Houston, TX., pay the interests, but live in peace. I love it.

■ Waiting for a period the Central Bank introduces Vatican Banking, Bank of the Canterbury, or Christian Exclusive Bank (CEB).

■ Some numbskulls actually believe that we may need Islamic Banking because it is practiced in the West too. So why not Gun Rights, because it is practiced in the West too?

Leadership lessons

■ Civilizations can only be understood by those who are civilized, (Alfred North Whitehead) - But just few minutes ago in the United States, House Speaker Nancy Pelosi in the most civilized comportment, handed her gavel to incoming Speaker John Boehner, ending a two-year democratic rule in Washington, and marking the beginning of Republican control. Is Nigeria's PDP learning from this movie?

CONFLICT RESOLUTION

■ "We can't solve problems by using the same kind of thinking we used when we created them," (Albert Einstein). But in Lagos, Governor Fashola has been begging doctors to call off a deadly strike; In Rivers, Judith, the wife of Governor Amechi has just begged doctors to call off a similar strike "for the interest of women and ". Would executive begging be some form of conflict resolution or conflict revolution?

CHANGE

■ We must become the change we want to see in the world," (Mohandas Gandhi) – No wonder, Jonathan, an underdog who claimed he went to school barefooted now trades in presidential jets; Buhari a diehard extremist who once crushed the Nation's constitution now preaches democracy; Ribadu, a self-acclaimed reformist who prosecuted corrupt politicians now runs under their pay roll, and feeds from their loots.

FOUNDING FATHERS AND TRIBAL LEADERS

■ Those who made significant intellectual contributions to the Constitution of the land, or fight selflessly for attainment of nationhood could pass for the "Founding Fathers" of that country. Major issue with early Nigerian political scholars is being unable to distinguish between Founding Fathers and Tribal Leaders.

FATHERHOOD AND NATIONHOOD

■ The psychological relevance of fatherhood diminishes when a father cannot provide for his family. Consequently, a nation loses the potency of nationhood when it cannot provide for her masses. When will Nigeria become a nation?

INDEPENDENCE

■ Independence is ability to do it on your own. Nigerian citizens, therefore, are fully independent, having to provide their water, lights; survive without roads, jobs, hospitals, schools, and other amenities. It's happy independence to those loving hard working citizens. Now…when will Nigeria as a country become independent?

CHOICE OF LEADERSHIP

■ But as voters, we have a preference that may not require a coin-toss, but some critical application of our thoughts. A choice between Obama's critical thinking, and Mitt Romney's policy blackout; I mean Mitt's incomprehensible strategy ambiguity that would return the country to failed Bush's policies that crashed our economy and hurt the middle class. Simply it's a choice between sugar-coated acid and spring water.

REFERENCES

A Vow to Respond. Current Events [serial online]. September 12, 2011;111(2):2. Available from: *Academic Search Complete,* Ipswich, MA.

Achebe, C. (1983). *The Trouble with Nigeria.* Heinemann Publisher.

Adeoye, A., (2010). How the British Planted the Seed of Disunity in Nigeria - *The African Courier.* www.theafricancourier.de/index.

Aluko, M. (2002). The Institutionalization of Corruption and Its Impact on Political Culture and Behavior in Nigeria. *Nordic Journal of African Studies 11*(3): 393-402 (2002)

Arikpo, A. B., Etor, R. B., & Usang, E. (2007). Development Imperatives for the Twenty-First Century In Nigeria. *Convergence, 40*(1/2), 55-65.

Aristotle. (n.d.). *BrainyQuote.com.* BrainyQuote.com

Atkins, P. B. & Parker, S. K. (2012). Understanding Individual Compassion in Organizations: The Role of Appraisals and Psychological Flexibility. *Academy Of Management Review, 37*(4), 524-546.

Bateman, T. S., & Snell, S. A. (2007). *Management: Leading and Collaborating in a Competitive World* (7th ed.). Boston, MA: McGraw-Hill/Irwin.

BBC (2010). Divide Nigeria in Two, Says Muammar Gaddafi. Tuesday, 16 March 2010. *news.bbc.co.*

Beamish, P.W., Morrison, A., Inkpen, A., & Rosenzweig, P. (2003). *International management:* Text and cases. (5th Ed.). Boston, MA: McGraw- Hill.

Burns, J. A. (1995). Transactional and Transformational Leadership. In J.T. Wren (ed.), *The leader's companion: Insights on leadership through the ages.* New York: The Free Press. [Reprinted courtesy of the *Journal of Contemporary Business*, 3(Autumn 1974) published by the School of Business Administration, University of Washington, Seattle, WA.

Chopra, P. K., & Kanji, G. K. (2010). Emotional intelligence: A catalyst for inspirational leadership and management excellence. *Total Quality Management & Business Excellence, 21*(10), 971-1004. doi:10.1080/14783363.2010.487704

Coawin R. G. (1972). Strategies for Organizational Innovation: an Empirical Comparison. *American SocMogical Review* 1972, Vol. 37 (August):441-454 EBSCOhost

Cooperrider, D.L. and L.E. Sekerka (2006), *'Toward a theory of positive organizational change',* in J.V.

Chuck Palahniuk. (n.d.). *BrainyQuote.* BrainyQuote.com.

Denney, R. L., &Wynkoop, T. F. (2000). Clinical neuropsychology in the criminal forensic setting. *Journal of Head Trauma Rehabilitation, 15,* 804–828.

Erich Fromm. (n.d.). *BrainyQuote.* BrainyQuote.com.

Feldman, R. (2003). *Epistemology.* Upper Saddle River, NJ: Prentice Hall.

Friedrich Nietzsche. (n.d.). *BrainyQuote.* BrainyQuote.com.

Freedman, Joshua M., Jensen, Anabel L., Rideout, Marsha C. (1998) *Handle With Care: Emotional Intelligence Activity Book.* Publisher: Six Seconds.

Gallos, J.V. (2006). *Organization development.* An Francisco, CA; Jossey-Bass.

Ghazinoory, S., Abdi, M., &Azadegan-Mehr, M. (2011). SWOT Methodology: A State-of-the-Art Review for the Past, a Framework for the Future. *Journal of Business Economics & Management, 12*(1), 24-48. doi:10.3846/16111699.2011.555358.

Gire J.T. (1999). A Psychological Analysis of Corruption in Nigeria. *Journal of Sustainable Development in Africa. Vol 1* No. 2, Summer 1999.

Golda Meir. (n.d.). *Brainy Quotes.* BrainyQuote.com.

Google.com (2012). Corporate Governance: Our Culture.

Harvey S. Firestone. (n.d.). *Brainy Quotes.* BrainyQuote.com.

Hickson, D. J., Hinings, C. R., Lee, C. A., Schneck, R. E., & Pennings, J. M. (1971). A Strategic Contingencies' Theory of Intraorganizational Power. *Administrative Science Quarterly, 16*(2), 216-229.

Hoopes, J. (2003). *False prophets. The gurus who created modern management and why their ideas are bad for business.* Cambridge, MA. Perseus.

Horrigan, Paul. G. (2005). Philosophy of Knowledge. www.horrigan.angelcities.com/knowledge2.htm

Ifidon, E. A. (2007). Unity without Unification: The Development of Nigeria's 'Inside-Out' Approach to African Political Integration, 1937-1963. *International Social Science Review, 82*(1/2), 39-54.

Institute for the Study of Violent Groups © 2012. Boko Haram.

International Monetary Fund December (2005) *Nigeria: Poverty Reduction Strategy Paper*

Johnson, P., & Duberley, J. (2000). *Understanding management research: An introduction to epistemology.* Thousand Oaks, CA: Sage Publications.

Jones, G.R. (2010). *Organizational theory, design, and change* (6th Ed.). Upper Saddle River, NJ: Prentice Hall.

Khan, H. I. (1914). Spiritual Liberty: Love, Human and Divine. The Philosophy of Love. Wahiduddin.net

King, D. T. (2003). USAID / Nigeria Economic Growth Activities Assessment; *Transition Period Summary Report* http://pdf.usaid.gov/pdf_docs/PDACG556.pdf

Kotter, J. P. (2006). Leading Change; Why Transformation Efforts Fail. *Harvard Business Review, 73*(2)

Koenig, M., & de Guchteneire, P. (2007). Political Governance of Cultural Diversity. *Democracy and Human Rights in Multicultural Societies* Intro.pdf

Kukah, M. H. (1993). *Religion, Politics, and Power in Northern Nigeria, Ibadan:* Spectrum Books.

Kuhn, T. S. (1962). *The Structure of Scientific Revolutions.* Second Edition, Enlarged, the University of Chicago Press, Chicago, 1970

Lawler, E. (2006). "Business Strategy: Creating the Winning Formula." *Organizational Development:* Josey-Bass, San Francisco, CA..

Locke, J. (1690). An essay concerning human understanding. www.ilt.columbia.edu/publications/Projects/digitexts/locke/understanding/chapter0233.html

Maja-Pearce, A. (2010). Nigeria's show of shame. *New African,* (498), 20.ebscohost

McAuley, J., Duberley, J. & Johnson, P. (2007). *Organization theory: Challenges and perspectives.* Upper Saddle River, NJ: Prentice Hall.

McFadden, C., Eakin, R., Beck-Frazier, S., & McGlone, J. (2005). Major approaches to the study of leadership. *Academic Exchange Quarterly, 9*(2), 71.

Miller, K. D., & Tsang, E. K. (2011). Testing management theories: critical realist philosophy and research methods. *Strategic Management Journal, 32*(2), 139-158.

Moser, P. K., & Vander Nat, A. (Eds.). (2003). *Human knowledge: Classical and contemporary approaches* (3rd ed.). New York, NY: Oxford University Press.

Musa, A. (2012). Socio-economic incentives, new media and the Boko Haram campaign of violence in Northern Nigeria. *Journal of African Media Studies, 4*(1), 111-124. doi:10.1386/jams.4.1.111_1

Nadler, David A., and Tushman Michael L. (1995). Beyond the Charismatic Leader: Leadership and Organizational Change. In J.T. Wren (ed.), *The leader's companion: Insights on leadership through the ages.* New York:

National Economic Empowerment and Development Strategy. *IMF Country Report* No. 05/433

Navahandi Afsaneh (2006). *The Art and Science of Leadership,* Fourth Edition, Published by Prentice Hall. Copyright © 2006, 2003, 2000, 1997 by *Pearson Education, Inc.*

Onadipe, A. (1999). Nigeria and Democracy: Third Time Lucky? *Contemporary Review, 275*(1603), 57.

Ogbo, A. (2008) Nigeria's Speaker swims in stormy Waters. *International Guardian.* www.guardiannews.us

Ogunbadejo, O. (1979) Conflict Images: Colonial Legacy, Ethnicity, and Corruption In Nigerian Politics, 1960-1966 *Utafiti-*Vol.4 No.1 Julv 1979

Ogunbiyi, T. (2012) Tackling The Menace Of Noise Pollution — *PM News Opinion.* pmnewsnigeria.com

OIC (2006) Charter of the Organization of the Islamic Conference. *Organization of the Islamic Conference.* http://www.oic-oci.org/is11/english/Charter-en.pdf

Plato. (n.d.). *BrainyQuote.* BrainyQuote.com.

Premeaux, S. (2009). The link between management behavior and ethical philosophy in the wake of the Enron convictions. *Journal of Business Ethics, 85*(1), 13-25.

Reuters, (2012) Sectarian violence kills more in Nigeria's Kaduna http://af.reuters.com/

Rogers, B., & Tresaugue M. (2008) TSU's Slade avoids prison with plea deal. *Houston Chronicle* - chron.com

Rosete, D., & Ciarrochi, J. (2005). Emotional Intelligence and its Relationship to Workplace Performance Outcomes of Leadership Effectiveness. *Leadership & Organization Development Journal, 26*(5/6), 388.

Salisu, M. (2000/006) Corruption in Nigeria . *Lancaster University Management School Working Paper* http://eprints.lancs.ac.uk/48533/1/Document.pdf

Schaubroeck, J. M., Hannah, S. T., Avolio, B. J., Kozlowski, S. W., Lord, R. G., Trevinño, L. K., & ... Peng, A. C. (2012). Embedding Ethical Leadership Within and Across Organization Levels. *Academy of Management Journal*, 55(5), 1053-1078.

Sulaiman, I. (1982) *A Revolution in History: The Jihad of Usman Dan Fodio.* Mansell Publishing Limited, London and New York.

Shuaibu, I. (2008) Nigeria: Generator Accident Kills Lawmaker. *This Day Newspaper,* Ed. 9/7/2008

Thomas Jefferson. (n.d.). BrainyQuote.com. *BrainyQuote* BrainyQuote.com

Tichy N. M., and Devanna M. A. (1990) *The Transformational Leader: The Key to Global Competitiveness,* 1e John Wiley & Sons, Inc.

Tom Robbins. (n.d.). *BrainyQuote* BrainyQuote.com.

United Nations Integrated Mission in Timor-Leste (2012) Democratic Governance; What is democratic Governance?

Usman dan Fodio. (2012). In *Encyclopædia Britannica.*

Victor Dike (2005) Corruption in Nigeria: A new paradigm for effective control. *Africa Economic Analysis, 2005* - anticorruptionleague.org

Santos, F. M., & Eisenhardt, K. M. (2005). Organizational Boundaries and Theories of Organization. *Organization Science, 16*(5), 491-508. doi:10.1287/orsc.1050.0152. EBSCO-HOST

Scott, W.R., Davis, G.F. (2007). Organizations and organizing. Upper Saddle River, NJ: *Prentice Hall.*

Shabazz, S. (2012). Nigeria ends oil subsidy national strike but will there be a civil war?. *New York Amsterdam News.* p. 2. EBSCOhost

Soyinka, W. (2007). The crimes of Buhari. Nigeriavillagesquare.com.

Yin, S. (2007).Objections surface over Nigerian census results - *Population Reference Bureau, 2007* - prb.org

Yunus, N., Ghazali, K., & Hassan, C. (2011). The influence of Leader's Emotional Intelligence: Mediating Effect of Leader-Member Exchange on Employees' Organizational Citizenship Behaviours. *Interdisciplinary Journal of Contemporary Research in Business, 3*(3), 1125-1134. EBSCOhost.

Zalta E., N. (Winter 2011 Edition), Edward N. Zalta (ed.), http://plato.stanford.edu/cgi-bin/encyclopedia/archinfo.cgi?entry=knowledge-value

PHOTO SOURCES

■ It would be hard to establish original sources of some images because they are either linked to multiple internet sources or retrieved from *International Guardian Photo Archives* .

AIRPORTS

ReviewNaija. http://www.review-naija.com/2012/07/murtala-muhammed-international-airport.html

Murtala Muhammed International Airport: Ahmet KOCAK 31 Aug 2006 http://www.geolocation.ws/v/P/1 5529093/nijerya-murtala-muhammed-havaalani/en

BRIBERY

Nigerian Police, bribery, fraud and corruption. http://www.gistmania.com/talk/topic,45266.0/imode.html

DANA CRASH

dailymail.co.uk . http://www.daily-mail.co.uk/news/article-2154149/Nigeria-plane-crash-kills-ALL-153-passengers-board-Dana-Air-flight.html

DELTA

http://www.sydneyairport.com.au/corporate/media-centre/multimedia-gallery/gallery-details?cat=%7B5C599F8C-5927-4727-8CE8-ED9B4C2C5ED2%7D

DR FRANCOIS DUVALIER

http://newssourceinfo.blogspot.com/2011_10_23_archive.html

IBORI

The guardian.co.uk:
http://www.guardian.co.uk/uk/2012/may/22/met-officers-nigerian-embezzler-conviction

MALNUTRITION

Academic Dictionaries and Encyclopedias. http://en.academic.ru/pictures/enwiki/83/Starved_girl.jpg

Associated Press. http://www.middle-townpress.com/articles/2010/12/29/news/doc4d1aa09bcf4840856 39793.txt

POWER GENERATOR

Naijalife Magazine:
http://naijalife.freehostia.com/mag/?p=827

SIR FREDERICK LUGARD

http://en.wikipedia.org/wiki/Frederick_Lugard,_1st_Baron_Lugard

SCHOOLS

Nigeria Infrastructure News (2011) State of Nigerian Roads: Across Four States. http://nigeriainfrastructure.blogspot.com/2011/11/across-four-states-state-of-our-roads.html

nairaland.com (2009) http://www.nairaland.com/1013860/state-should-start-out-state

UNESCO Youth Ambassador for the Culture of Peace (2011). A Ray of Hope,

http://arayofhopeunesco.blogspot.com/2011_06_01_archive.html

Ian Attfield Education Adviser, Tanzania.
http://blogs.dfid.gov.uk/2010/02/jigawa-surges-up-the-education-spending-league/

YAKUBU-GOWON

http://www.lifestories.spruz.com/pt/YAKUBU-GOWON-NIGERIAS-BLOODIEST-RULER/blog.htm